Coleção
Eu gosto m@is

ENSINO FUNDAMENTAL

Edgar Laporta

INGLÊS

8º ano

1ª EDIÇÃO
SÃO PAULO
2012

IBEP

Coleção Eu Gosto Mais
Inglês 8º ano
© IBEP, 2012

Diretor superintendente	Jorge Yunes
Gerente editorial	Célia de Assis
Editor	Angelo Gabriel Rozner
Assistente editorial	Fernanda dos Santos Silva
Revisão técnica	Mariett Regina R. de Azevedo
Revisão	Rachel Prochoroff Castanheira
Coordenadora de arte	Karina Monteiro
Assistente de arte	Marilia Vilela
	Tomás Troppmair
Coordenadora de iconografia	Maria do Céu Pires Passuello
Assistente de iconografia	Adriana Neves
	Wilson de Castilho
Ilustrações	José Luis Juhas
Produção editorial	Paula Calviello
Produção gráfica	José Antônio Ferraz
Assistente de produção gráfica	Eliane M. M. Ferreira
Projeto gráfico e capa	Departamento de arte IBEP
Editoração eletrônica	Formato Comunicação

CIP-BRASIL. CATALOGAÇÃO-NA-FONTE
SINDICATO NACIONAL DOS EDITORES DE LIVROS, RJ

L32i

Laporta, Edgar
  Inglês : 8º ano / Edgar Laporta. - 1.ed. - São Paulo : IBEP, 2012.
  il. ; 28 cm.   (Eu gosto mais)

  ISBN 978-85-342-3446-7 (aluno) - 978-85-342-3450-4 (mestre)

  1. Língua inglesa - Estudo e ensino (Ensino fundamental). I. Título. II. Série.

12-6212   CDD: 372.6521
                                                 CDU: 373.3.016=111

28.08.12   05.09.12   038547

1ª edição - São Paulo - 2012
Todos os direitos reservados

IBEP

Av. Alexandre Mackenzie, 619 - Jaguaré
São Paulo - SP - 05322-000 - Brasil - Tel.: (11) 2799-7799
www.editoraibep.com.br   editoras@ibep-nacional.com.br

Impressão Serzegraf - Setembro 2016

Apresentação

O inglês é um idioma de grande importância no mundo globalizado de hoje. Está presente em nossa vida diária, na TV, no cinema, na Internet, nas músicas, nos livros, nas revistas etc.

Há muito tempo, tornou-se um dos principais meios de comunicação no turismo, no comércio mundial, nas competições esportivas, nos congressos sobre ciência e tecnologia, nos meios diplomáticos, nos encontros de líderes mundiais etc. Por isso, cada vez mais pessoas estudam e falam inglês.

Com o objetivo de despertar em você o gosto pelo idioma inglês, tivemos a preocupação de abordar textos variados e que se relacionam com sua vida.

As atividades de interpretação dos textos levam você a ler e reler o texto para encontrar as respostas adequadas às perguntas.

Sempre que você tiver alguma dificuldade em descobrir o sentido de palavras ou expressões do texto, lembre-se de que há no final do livro o vocabulário geral para ajudá-lo.

As noções de gramática são apresentadas na seção *Learn this* de forma simples e abreviada. Logo a seguir, você vai treiná-las com exercícios rápidos e simples.

Participe ativamente das aulas e aproveite esta oportunidade para aprender inglês.

O autor

Sumário

Lesson 1 – Simple present tense, Interrogative form (do, does) 7

Dialogue: *An American tourist in Rio* 7
- Text comprehension 9
- Learn this 9
- Activities 10

Lesson 2 – Simple present negative form (do not, does not) 13

Dialogue: *Do you speak English?* 13
- Text comprehension 14
- Learn this 14
- Activities 15
- Role-play – oral drill 18
- Review 19
- Fun time 21

Lesson 3 – Modal verb may; possessive adjectives 23

Dialogue: *May I play with you?* 23
- Text comprehension 24
- Learn this 25
- Activities 26

Lesson 4 – Regular verbs, use of do, do not, does, does not 28

Dialogue: *I help my parents in the kitchen* 28
- Text comprehension 29

- Learn this 30
- Activities 31
- Role-play – oral drill 33
- Let's sing 33

Lesson 5 – Interrogative pronouns: which, where 34

Dialogue: *Why don't you talk to me?* 34
- Text comprehension 35
- Activities 36
- Review 37
- Fun time 39

Lesson 6 – Genitive case; interrogative pronoun whose 41

Dialogue: *Lost and found* 41
- Text comprehension 42
- Learn this 43
- Activities 43

Lesson 7 – Possessive adjectives; Possessive pronoun; interrogative whose 45

Dialogue: *Whose dog is this?* 45
- Text comprehension 46
- Learn this 46
- Activities 47
- Role-play – oral drill 48

Lesson 8 – Model verb can, cannot/ can't, could **49**

Text: *Whe can enjoy life in contact with nature* . **49**

    Text comprehension 50

    Learn this 50

    Activities 51

    Review 52

    Fun time 54

Lesson 9 – Modal verbs: need to – have to – must **55**

Text: *I must, you must...* **55**

    Text comprehension 56

    Learn this 56

    Activities 57

Lesson 10 – Past tense of regular verbs **58**

Text: *Old times x modern times* **58**

    Text comprehension 59

    Learn this 59

    Activities 60

Lesson 11 – Past tense of Regular and Irregular verbs **61**

Text: *Saint Peter's farm* **61**

    Text comprehension 64

    Learn this 64

    Activities 65

    Fun time 67

    Listen and write – Dictation 70

    Fun time 70

Lesson 12 – Past tense of regular verbs; interrogative and negative forms **71**

Text: *Did you buy some dessert* **71**

    Text comprehension 72

    Learn this 72

    Activities 73

Lesson 13 – Past tense of irregular verbs **74**

Text: *Reasons for a long life* **74**

    Text comprehension 75

    Learn this 75

    Activities 76

Lesson 14 – Past tense; interrogative form, irregular verbs **77**

Dialogue: *Did you have a nice vacation?* **77**

    Text comprehension 78

    Learn this 79

    Activities 79

    Fun time 81

    Review 82

Lesson 15 – Past tense; negative form; irregular verbs 83

Dialogue: *At the Police Station* 83

    Text comprehension 84

    Learn this 84

    Activities 85

Lesson 16 – Irregular verbs: past tense, interrogative and negative form 86

Text: *Catch the thief!* 86

    Text comprehension 88

    Learn this 89

    Activities 90

    Learn this 90

    Fun time 94

    Let's sing 94

Lesson 17 – Regular and Irregular verbs affirmative, negative and interrogative form 95

Text: *Nancy and Jeff* 95

    Text comprehension 96

    Activities 97

    Fun time 97

Lesson 18 – Asking questions giving answers 98

Text: *Why...? Because...* 98

    Learn this 100

    Activities 101

    Fun time 102

Lesson 19 – Interrogative words 104

Text: *Conversation in a school* 104

    Learn this 105

    Activities 105

    Let's sing 108

List of irregular verbs 109

General vocabulary 110

Lesson 1

SIMPLE PRESENT TENSE: INTERROGATIVE FORM (DO, DOES)

Do you speak English?

Yes, I do.

An American tourist in Rio

Tourist: Taxi, please!
Taxi driver: Yes?
Tourist: Do you speak English?
Taxi driver: Yes, I do, but I have hearing difficulty. Can you speak up, please?
Tourist: Sure! I'm an American tourist. My wife and I want to visit some attractive places in Rio. Are you available?
Taxi driver: Sure! I'm entirely at your disposal. I can show you the statue of Christ, the Redeemer, on the Corcovado, Sugar Loaf, the beaches of Copacabana, Ipanema... I can take you to shopping malls, stores, restaurants, soccer stadiums, museums... If you want, I can take you farther: I can take you to Búzios, Petrópolis, Cabo Frio... where nature is simply wonderful.
Tourist: OK! How much do you charge for your service?
Taxi driver: One hundred and sixty dollars a day.
Tourist: That's OK. It's neither cheap nor expensive. But pay attention not to drive through dangerous places...
Taxi driver: Don't be afraid. I avoid dangerous places. Let's begin our tour by the beaches...
Tourist: It's a good idea!

8 eight

TEXT COMPREHENSION

1 Who calls a taxi? _____

2 Does the taxi driver speak English? _____

3 Is the taxi driver busy or available? _____

4 The taxi driver asks the tourist to: ( ) speak low   ( ) speak up

5 The driver's charge is
   ( ) cheap   ( ) expensive   ( ) neither cheap nor expensive

6 The American tourist asks the taxi driver
   ( ) to drive through dangerous places
   ( ) to avoid dangerous places

7 The tour begins
   ( ) by the beaches
   ( ) by the stadium of Maracanã

LEARN THIS

Do/does

Quando fazemos perguntas no **simple present**, com verbos não auxiliares, usamos **do** ou **does**. **Do** e **does** também aparecem em respostas curtas (**short answers**) substituindo o sentido dos verbos das perguntas.

Observe a conjugação de verbos na forma interrogativa e seguida de resposta curta (**short answer**) na forma afirmativa:

– **Do**   **you speak English?**   (– Você fala inglês?)   –**Yes, I do**.   (– Sim, eu falo.)

              he speak English?   (– Ele fala inglês?)   –**Yes, he does**.   (– Sim, ele fala?)

– **Does**   **she speak English?**   (– Ela fala inglês?)   –**Yes, she does**. (– Sim, ela fala?)

– **Do you like Rio?** (– Você gosta do Rio?)   –**Yes, we do**.   (– Sim, nós gostamos.)

– **Do they like Rio?** (– Será que eles gostam do Rio?)   –**Yes, they do**.   (– Sim, eles/elas gostam.)

Nota:
O verbo **to do** como auxiliar não tem tradução. A palavra **do** indica que a pergunta está sendo feita no tempo presente com uma das pessoas verbais: **I, you, we, they**.

Does é usado na 3ª pessoa do singular do presente do indicativo:

Do I... ? (Do I speak fluently?)	Do we...? (Do we drive cars?)
Do you...? (Do you live in Rio?)	Do you...? (Do you like samba?)
Does he...? (Does he speak fluently?)	Do they...? (Do they speak Spanish?)
Does she ...? (Does she speak fluently?)	Do they...? (Do they speak fluently?)
Does it...? (Does it love bones?) (the dog)	Do they...? (Do they love bones? (the dogs)

Quando usamos **does**, o verbo principal fica na forma básica (sem o **s**).
Observe:
Mary loves John.
Does Mary love John?

ACTIVITIES

1 Complete the dialogue with do or does:

a) _____ she like flowers?

Yes she _____ . She likes flowers very much.

b) _____ you like coconut water?

Yes, I _____ . I like coconut water. It's delicious.

c) _____ your wife like hot weather?

Yes, she _____ . She loves hot weather.

d) _____ you like Brazilian people?

Yes, I _____ . Brazilian people are very friendly.

2 Write do or does. Use does in the third person singular:

a) _____ they speak English?

b) _____ you understand me?

c) _____ Nancy live in France?

d) _____ they go to Búzios today?

e) _____ you want to visit Corcovado?

f) _____ she like coffee?

g) _____ Mary dance well?

3) Complete the dialogues with do or does:

_____ you like ice cream?

Yes, I _____. I like ice cream!

_____ you like sports?

Yes, I _____. I like sports!

_____ she dance well?

Yes, she _____. She dances well.

_____ Bob love Jane?

Yes, he _____. He loves Jane.

_____ they work hard?

Yes, they _____. They work hard!

4) Write do or does. Use does in the third person singular:

a) _____ you know my parents?

b) _____ they study English?

c) _____ she dance well?

d) _____ you like movies?

e) _____ Bob live here?

f) _____ you drink coffee?

g) _____ that bird sing?

eleven **11**

5 Change the sentences to the interrogative form:
(Atenção: o verbo principal permanece sempre na forma básica, na forma interrogativa.)

a) You speak English. _____

b) She speaks English. _____

c) They speak English. _____

d) He likes coffee. _____

e) They go to Búzios. _____

f) She goes to Búzios. _____

6 Change the sentences to the third (3rd) person singular in the interrogative form:

a) Do they like classical music? (She)
_____

b) Do you understand me? (Jane)
_____

c) Do they play football? (She)
_____

d) Do you want to drink coconut water? (She)
_____

e) Do they take the bags to the hotel? (He)
_____

f) Do the tourists visit attractive places? (tourist)
_____

7 Answer the questions in the third person singular. Follow the example:

a) Does the tourist like Brazil?
Yes, he does.
He likes Brazil.

b) Does your friend go to the United States?
_____
_____

c) Does the tourist speak English well?
_____
_____

12 twelve

Lesson 2

SIMPLE PRESENT NEGATIVE FORM (DO NOT, DOES NOT)

Do you speak English?

An American meets a Frenchman in a street in Rome and they begin to talk.

American: Good evening!
Frenchman: Good evening!
American: May I ask you some questions?
Frenchman: Sure!
American: Where are you from?
Frenchman: I'm from France.
American: Do you speak English?
Frenchman: I don't speak English well. And you, where are you from?
American: I'm from America. I'm American.
Frenchman: Do you speak French?
American: Just a little bit!
Frenchman: I have a good suggestion to improve our communication, you help me learn English and I can help you learn French while we visit tourist attractions in Rome.
American: OK! That's a good idea! Then let's go round Rome together!

TEXT COMPREHENSION

1 The American meets the Frenchman:

( ) in a shop ( ) in a square ( ) on a street

2 Does the American speak French?

_____

3 Does the Frenchman speak English well?

_____

_____

4 Where are the American and the French tourists?

They are in a street in _____.

5 What are they doing in Rome?

_____

6 Who presents a good suggestion to improve their communication?

_____

7 Complete:

The Frenchman suggestion consist of: the American helps the Frenchman learn _____ and the Frenchman _____.

LEARN THIS

Usamos o verbo **to do** em frases interrogativas e negativas com verbos comuns (não auxiliares). No forma negativa do presente do indicativo usamos **does not** ou **doesn't** para a 3ª pessoa do singular e **do not** ou **don't** para as demais pessoas verbais.

VERB TO LIKE – SIMPLE PRESENTE			
Affirmative form	**Tradução**	**Negative full form**	**Negative contracted form**
I like	(Eu gosto)	I do not like	I don't like
You like	(Você gosta)	You do not like	You don't like
He likes	(Ele gosta)	He does not like	He doesn't like
She likes	(Ela gosta)	She does not like	She doesn't like
It likes	(Ele/ela gosta)	It does not like	It doesn't like
We like	(Nós gostamos)	We do not like	We don't like
You like	(Vocês gostam)	You do not like	You don't like
They like	(Eles/elas gostam)	They do not like	They don't like

ACTIVITIES

1 Complete the answers in the negative form:

Do you like fish?

No, I don't. I don't like fish.

Do you speak English?

No, _____. _____ speak English.

Do you swim?

No, _____. I _____ swim!

Do you drive well?

Yes, I do. But they _____. They _____ drive well.

Do you live in a flat?

No, I _____. I live in a house.

Does she like you?

No, she doesn't. She _____ like me.

2 Look at the example and do the same according to the picture:

a) want – sandwich/pizza
   Do you want a sandwich? No, I don't. I prefer pizza.

b) want – soup/sandwich

c) want – some salad/a hot dog.

d) like – coffee/orange juice

e) play – tennis/to play soccer

3 Write **do not** or **does not**:

a) I _____ live in São Paulo.

b) She _____ dance well.

c) We _____ like lemons.

d) You _____ speak English.

e) He _____ live in a flat.

f) Bob _____ sing well.

g) Mary _____ drive cars.

h) I _____ eat bananas.

i) Paul and Mary _____ understand English.

j) I _____ feel well.

4 Change to the negative form.
Use the contracted form – **don't** or **doesn't**:

a) **I go to the movies.**
I don't go to the movies.

b) She loves you.
_____

c) I understand English.
_____

d) They know Brazil.
_____

e) I eat cheese and eggs in the morning.
_____

f) I drink coffee in the morning.
_____

g) I study at night.
_____

h) She lives in a house.
_____

i) Peter works in a factory.
_____

5 Follow the pattern:

a) **(like coffee – prefer tea).**
Do you like coffee?
No, I don't like coffee. I prefer tea.

b) (like ham – prefer cheese)
_____
_____

c) (like Coca-Cola – prefer lemonade)
_____
_____

d) (like to live in the city – prefer to live in the country)
_____
_____

seventeen 17

ROLE-PLAY – ORAL DRILL

You can ask questions to a classmate and he/she answers. Use the words in the box below and ask questions to a classmate.

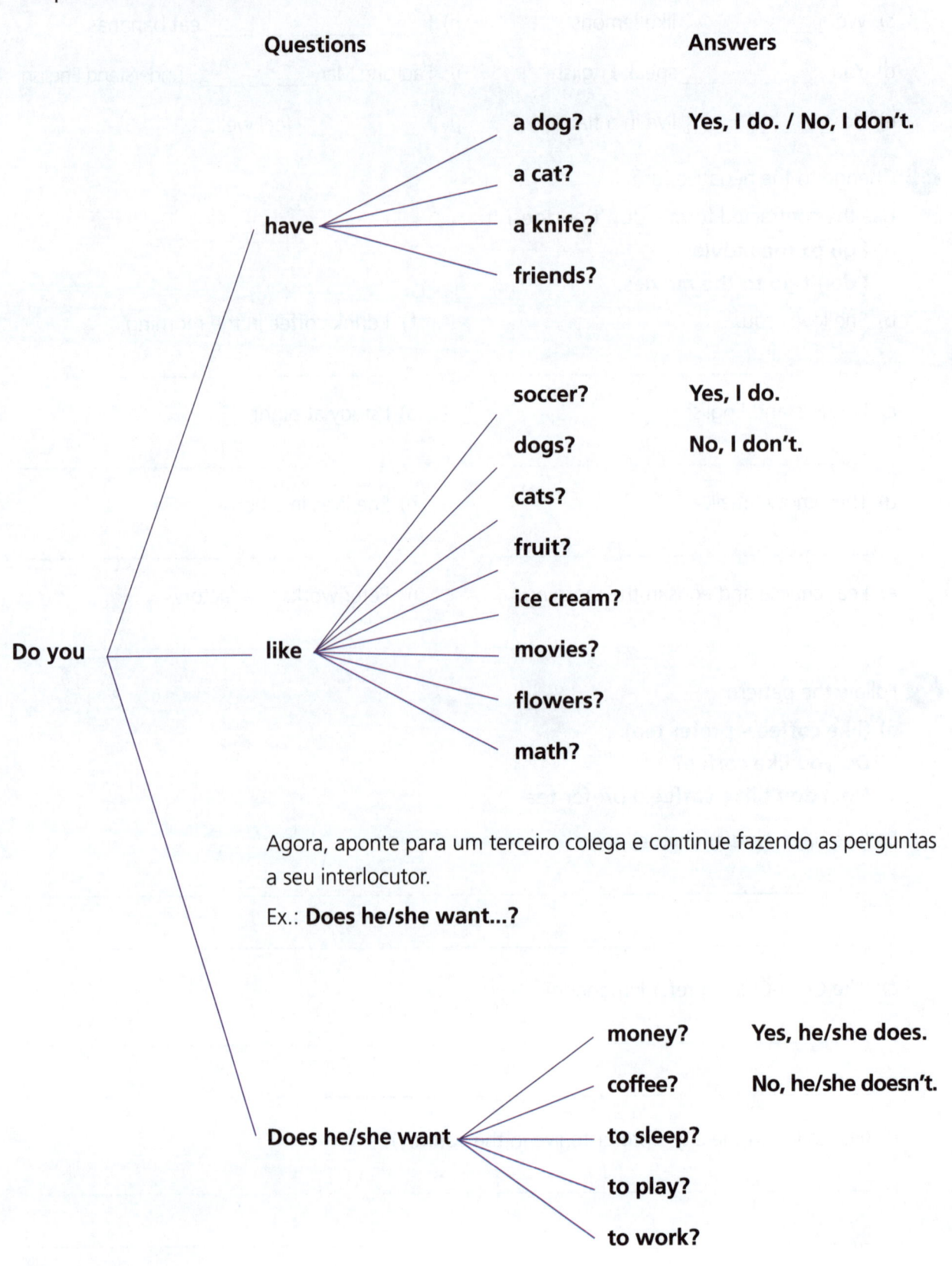

Questions   **Answers**

Do you — **have**
- a dog?
- a cat?
- a knife?
- friends?

Yes, I do. / No, I don't.

Do you — **like**
- soccer?
- dogs?
- cats?
- fruit?
- ice cream?
- movies?
- flowers?
- math?

Yes, I do.
No, I don't.

Agora, aponte para um terceiro colega e continue fazendo as perguntas a seu interlocutor.

Ex.: **Does he/she want...?**

Does he/she want
- money?
- coffee?
- to sleep?
- to play?
- to work?

Yes, he/she does.
No, he/she doesn't.

REVIEW

1 Change into the interrogative form:
   a) You drive well.
   Do you drive well?
   b) They study at night.

   c) They want to eat now.

   d) You get up early.

   e) They go to bed late.

   f) You speak English.

   g) They want some orange juice.

   h) You sleep well.

   i) They live here.

2 Change into the interrogative form:
   a) She knows John.
   Does she know John?
   b) She buys a magazine.

   c) Your father works hard.

   d) She lives in Rio.

   e) He needs money.

   f) Mary dances well.

   g) Monica loves Marcel.

   h) She pays attention to class.

nineteen **19**

3) Change into the negative form:

a) **You drive well.**
You do not (don't) drive well.

b) They study at night.
_____

c) They want to eat now.
_____

d) I get up early.
_____

e) We go to bed late.
_____

4) Change into the negative form:

a) **She buys magazines.**
She does not (doesn't) buy magazines.

b) My father works in a factory.
_____

c) She lives in Rio.
_____

d) My cousin needs money.
_____

e) Jane dances well.
_____

f) Margareth loves a tall boy.
_____

g) She pays attention to class.
_____

5) Answer negatively. Follow the pattern:

a) **Do you study at night?**
(in the morning)
No, I don't. I study in the morning.

b) Do you get up early? (late)
_____

c) Do you go to bed late? (early)
_____

d) Do you speak English? (Portuguese)
_____

e) Do you want coffee? (tea)
_____

f) Do you help your mother? (my sister)
_____

FUN TIME

1 Three-letters crosswords

cow – man – hen – dog – fox – bus – pen – egg – box – bed – sun – car – cat – hat – boy

a)

b)

c)

d)

2 Four-letters words

a)

b)

c)

d)

e)

twenty-one **21**

3 Fruit – colors – animals – nature
Observe the pictures and write their names according to the following order:

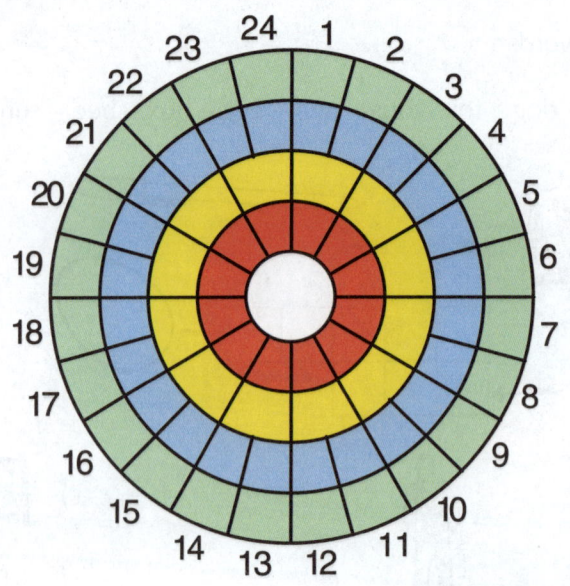

Fruit names
Green circle
Begin at number 1.

Colors names
Blue circle
Begin at number 1.

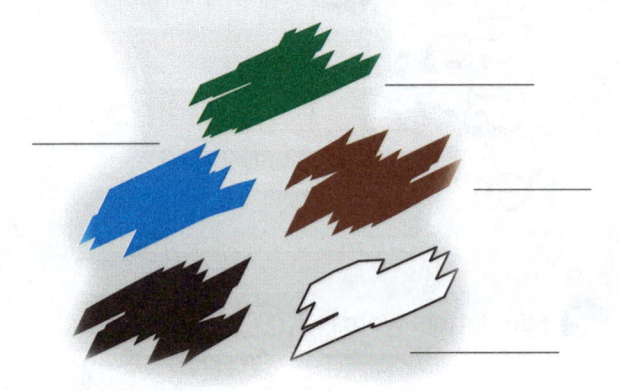

Animal names
Yellow circle

Nature names
Red circle

22   twenty-two

Lesson 3

MODAL VERB MAY:
POSSESSIVE ADJECTIVES

May I play with you?

The bell is ringing...
Ralph: Who's at the door?
Colin: It's me, Colin. May I play with you, Ralph?
Ralph: Of course! Come in.
Do you like computer games?
Colin: Of course!
Ralph: Then let's go to my bedroom.
Damn it! The electric cord of my computer is not here!
Dad, where is the electric cord of my computer?
Dad: Look for it in your sister's bedroom.
Ralph: It is not in her bedroom.
Dad: Look for it in your brother's bedroom.
Ralph: It is not in his bedroom.
Mom, where is the electric cord of my computer?
Mom: The electric cord... The electric cord is here in the backyard.
Ralph: Oh, mom!!!
Mom: Excuse me, Ralph. The clothes line was broken...

TEXT COMPREHENSION

1 How many people take part in this dialogue?
_____

2 Who are they?
_____

3 Colin goes to Ralph's house:
( ) to study   ( ) to play   ( ) to eat

4 Does Colin like computer games? _____

5 Ralph invites Colin to play
( ) in the backyard   ( ) in his bedroom

6 Ralph looks for the electric cord
( ) in his bedroom   ( ) in his father's bedroom
( ) in his sister's bedroom   ( ) in his brother's bedroom

7 Complete:
The mother takes the electric cord from the computer because the clothes _____ broken.

8 Where is the electric cord? _____

9 Write the words or expressions in the box under the appropriate pictures:

> backyard – electric cord – to play – bedroom – clothes line – the bell rings

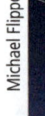

24 twenty-four

LEARN THIS

1. **Possessive adjectives**

VERB TO HAVE – SIMPLE PRESENT TENSE		
Personal pronouns	**Possessive adjectives**	**Examples**
I	My	I have a car. My car is white.
You	Your	You have a dog. Your dog is a terrier.
He	His	He speaks English. His English is perfect.
She	Her	She has two sons. Her sons are twins.
It	Its	The tree is big. Its leaves are green.
We	Our	We have a grandfather. Our grandfather is ill.
You	Your	You have sisters. Your sisters are nice.
They	Their	They have bikes. Their bikes are blue.

2. **Verb may**

O verbo **may** é um **modal verb**, isto é, tem a função de auxiliar do verbo principal e geralmente é empregado para pedir licença ou permissão formal. Também pode indicar escolha. Veja os exemplos.

a) Permissão:

May I come in? (Posso entrar?)

May I sit on that chair? (Posso sentar naquela cadeira?)

b) Escolha:

You may stay at home or go to the beach. (Você pode ficar em casa ou ir à praia).

3. Uso de **do** e **does**:

Veja o esquema da forma interrogativa com verbos comuns (não auxiliares):

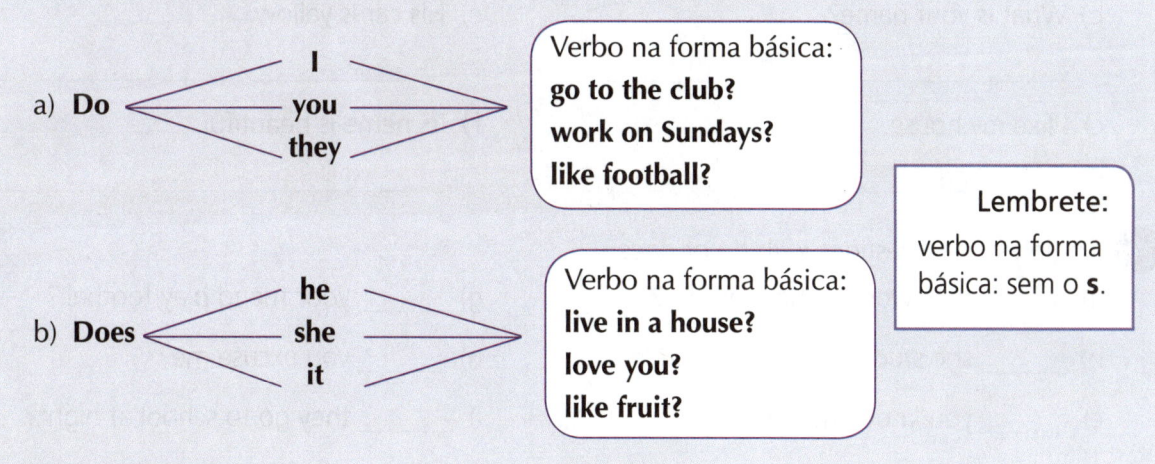

a) **Do** I / you / they → Verbo na forma básica:
go to the club?
work on Sundays?
like football?

b) **Does** he / she / it → Verbo na forma básica:
live in a house?
love you?
like fruit?

Lembrete: verbo na forma básica: sem o **s**.

4. Mom = mother
Dad = father
Mom, **dad** são tratamentos carinhosos para mãe e pai.

twenty-five **25**

ACTIVITIES

1 Conjugate the verb to live (morar, viver), changing the possessives according to the personal pronouns:

I live in my house.

You _____

He _____

She _____

It _____

We _____

You _____

They _____

2 Write in the plural. Look at the model:

a) **His book is new. Her book is new, too.**
   Their books are new.

b) His house is modern. Her house is modern, too.
   _____

c) His car is red. Her car is red, too.
   _____

d) His teacher is good. Her teacher is good, too.
   _____

e) His watch is imported. Her watch is imported, too.
   _____

3 Change into the plural form. Follow the pattern:

a) **Where is your book?**
   Where are your books?

b) What is your name?
   _____

c) I like my house.
   _____

d) Her blouse is red.
   _____

e) His car is yellow.
   _____

f) Its name is beautiful.
   _____

4 Complete the questions with do or does:

a) _____ they work in the morning?

b) _____ she study near her house?

c) _____ you know my parents?

d) _____ she love you?

e) _____ you speak English?

f) _____ Mariana get up early?

g) _____ your friend play football?

h) _____ you excuse me?

i) _____ they go to school at night?

j) _____ you like video games?

k) _____ Mike and Jim live near your house?

l) _____ Jenny go to school by bus?

5 Ask questions for these answers. (Use do or does).

a) Do you play video games with your friend?
   Yes, I play video games with my friend.

b) _____
   Yes, I do. I like fruit.

c) _____
   Yes, she does. She likes fruit.

d) _____
   Yes, they do. They play football on Saturdays.

e) _____
   No, I don't. I don't know England.

f) _____
   No, she doesn't. She doesn't know England.

g) _____
   No, they don't. They don't live in a house.

h) _____
   No, she doesn't. She doesn't go with me.

6 Nessa atividade você vai pedir várias licenças ao professor. Sirva-se das palavras ou expressões do quadro.

Dica: Comece seus pedidos com a expressão: **May I...?**

> come in – to the – toilet – go out – to my – water
> go – classmate – drink – stand up – speak

a) Posso entrar?
   _____

b) Posso sair?
   _____

c) Posso ir ao toalete?
   _____

d) Posso sair para beber água?
   _____

e) Posso ficar de pé?
   _____

f) Posso falar com meu colega?
   _____

Lesson 4

REGULAR VERBS, USE OF DO, DO NOT, DOES, DOES NOT

I help my parents in the kitchen

Reporter: Do you help your parents in the kitchen?
Jason: Yes, I do.
Reporter: Do you sweep the kitchen?
Jason: No, I don't.
Reporter: Do you wash the dishes, the glasses, the cups?
Jason: No, I don't.
Reporter: Do you peel the potatoes?
Jason: No, I don't peel the potatoes.
Reporter: Do you set the table?
Jason: No, I don't set the table.
Reporter: Do you like to cook?
Jason: No, I don't like to cook.
Reporter: Explain to me, what do you like to do in the kitchen?
Jason: I like to eat!!!

TEXT COMPREHENSION

1 According to the text, connect the actions to the pictures:
A) Jason doesn't like

a) to peel the potatoes

b) to set the table

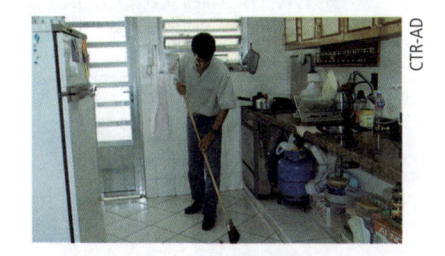

c) to cook

d) to wash the dishes, the cups, the glasses

e) to sweep the kitchen

2 Which is the odd word?

| living room | dining room | clothes |
| kitchen | bedroom | bathroom |

twenty-nine **29**

3 Complete the sentences using the words from the box. (You can add new words if you want.)

> kitchen, living room, oranges, onions, bread, meat, vegetables, car, clothes, street, sidewalk, hands, dog, cake, plates, glasses, beans, manioc, pineapples, macaroni, spaghetti, pizza, sausages

a) What can you peel?

I can peel potatoes, onions, peaches, _____

_____

b) My mother can cook eggs, meat, _____

_____

c) We can eat _____

_____

d) He washes the car, _____

_____

e) I sweep the room, _____

_____

LEARN THIS

AFFIRMATIVE/NEGATIVE/INTERROGATIVE FORM OF REGULAR VERBS

–**Do you wash the plates?** (–Você lava os pratos?)

–**No, I don't. I don't wash the plates.** (–Não, eu não lavo. Eu não lavo os pratos.)

É obrigatório o uso do verbo **to do** em frases interrogativas e negativas com verbos comuns (não auxiliares).

Observe a conjugação do verbo **to like** (gostar) no presente do indicativo:

Affirmative form	Interrogative form
I like (eu gosto)	**Do I like?**
You like (você gosta)	**Do you like?**
He likes (ele gosta)	**Does he like?**
She likes (ela gosta)	**Does she like?**
It likes (ele/ela gosta)	**Does it like?**
We like (nós gostamos)	**Do we like?**
You like (vocês gostam)	**Do you like?**
They like (eles/elas gostam)	**Do they like?**

Negative form (full form)	Negative form (contracted form)
I do not like	I don't like
You do not like	You don't like
He does not like	He doesn't like
She does not like	She doesn't like
It does not like	It doesn't like
We do not like	We don't like
You do not like	You don't like
They do not like	They don't like

ACTIVITIES

1 Answer (according to the text) in the third person singular:
   a) **Does Jason sweep the kitchen?**
      No, he doesn't. He doesn't sweep the kitchen.

   b) Does Jason wash the dishes?

   c) Does he wash the glasses, the cups?

   d) Does he peel the potatoes?

   e) Does he set the table?

   f) Does he like to cook?

   g) Does he like to eat?

2 Answer affirmatively. Follow the pattern:
   a) **Do you work in a factory?** Yes, I do. I work in a factory.

   b) Do you speak English?

   c) Do you live in Rio?

   d) Do you need money?

   e) Do you write letters?

thirty-one **31**

3 Answer affirmatively. Follow the pattern:

a) **Does she sleep late?**   **Yes, she does. She sleeps late.**

b) Does he smoke cigarettes? _____

c) Does she play the piano well? _____

d) Does Bob like school? _____

4 Answer negatively. Follow the pattern:

a) **Do you work hard?**
No, I don't. I don't work hard.

b) Do you sleep early?

_____

c) Do you speak French?

_____

d) Do you drink coffee?

_____

e) Does she like fish?

_____

f) Does she dance well?

_____

5 Change into interrogative and negative forms:

a) **You understand English.**
Do you understand English? You don't understand English.

b) They play soccer.

_____

c) She works in a shop.

_____

d) You get up early.

_____

e) Jane sells clothes.

_____

f) He buys old cars.

_____

6 Listen and write the missing words:

– _____ help _____ parents?

– Yes, _____

– _____ to cook?

– No, I don't.

– I like, _____

ROLE-PLAY – ORAL DRILL

You can ask questions to a classmate and he/she answers.
See the examples A) B) and C):
Pergunte se ele(a) gosta de algo.

A) **Do you like potatoes, orange, fruit juice, ice cream, lemonade?**
   O(a) colega responde afirmando que gosta:
   – **Yes, I do. I like…**

B) **Do you like… to cook? / to sweep the kitchen? / to wash the plates? / to set the table?**
   O(a) colega responde negando:
   – **No, I don't like to…**

C) **Do you like… (lemon? – coffee? – fish? – potatoes?)**
   O colega responde negando e dizendo que detesta. (**I hate…**):
   – **No, I don't like… I hate…**

LET'S SING

In the kitchen

My girlfriend is in the kitchen,
And I am in the kitchen, too.
My girlfriend, my love, my dear,
Let's cook for me and you.

You are hungry
And I am hungry, too.
My love, the dinner is burning!
And my heart is burning, too!

Antes de cantar a música, ouça o professor ou o CD, prestando atenção na pronúncia das palavras. Procure, também, saber o significado delas

Lesson 5

INTERROGATIVE PRONOUNS: WHICH, WHERE

*Jessica, I like you very much!
I'd like to meet you
after class.
I have so many things
to tell you...
Please say yes
and make me happy.
From your admirer,
Andrew.*

Why don't you talk to me?

Andrew: I don't know what to do. I like a beautiful blond girl in my class, but she doesn't talk to me.
Paul: Why don't you send a message to her? I may deliver it to you.
Andrew: It's a good idea. (And Andrew writes a lovely message to Jessica.)
Andrew: Paul, here is the message. Can you give it to Jessica?
Paul: Sure! Tomorrow morning at school.
Andrew: Thank you. You are a good friend.

The next day ...

Paul: Jessica, take this, please. It is from one of your friends.
Jessica: Thank you.

TEXT COMPREHENSION

Answer according to the text:

1 What is the matter with Andrew? _____

2 Who helps Andrew? _____

3 What is Paul's suggestion?

( ) To call Jessica by telephone.

( ) To write a message to Jessica.

( ) To go to school and talk to her.

4 Does Andrew agree Paul's suggestion? _____

5 Jessica is:

( ) a funny blond girl.

( ) a beautiful blond girl.

( ) a nice blond girl.

6 What is Andrew's message to Jessica? Write it:

_____
_____
_____
_____
_____
_____
_____
_____

7 When is Paul going to deliver the message?

_____

8 Where is Paul going to deliver the message?

_____

9 Is Paul a good friend?

_____

thirty-five **35**

ACTIVITIES

1 Look at the diagram and at the example and complete the sentences according to the pictures:

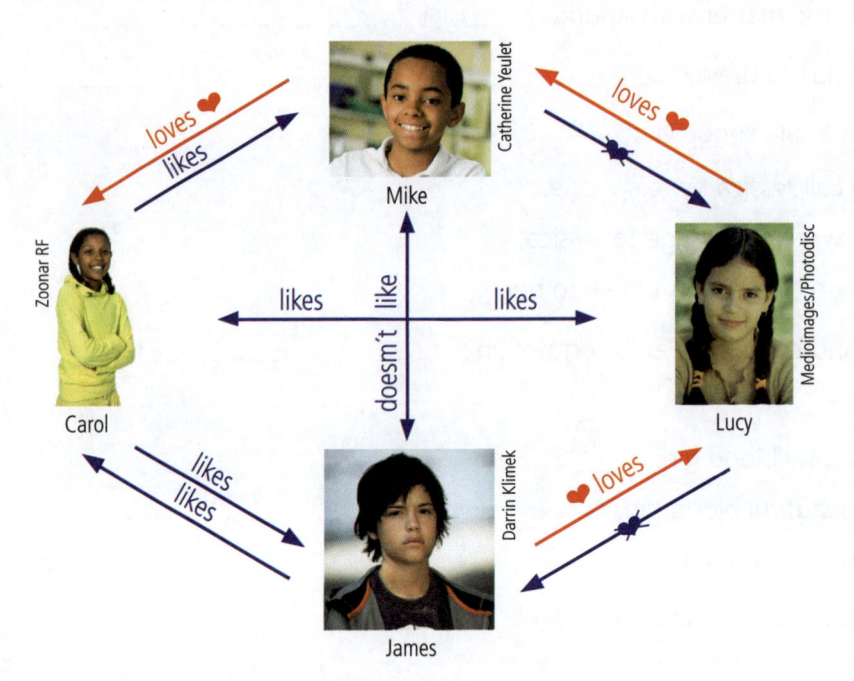

See the example:

Mike doesn't love Lucy. Lucy loves Mike.

a) Lucy loves Mike, but Mike doesn't love Lucy.

b) James _____ Lucy, but Lucy _____ James.

c) Mike _____ Carol. Carol _____ Mike.

d) Carol and James _____ each other.

e) Carol and Lucy _____ each other.

f) James _____ Mike.

g) Mike _____ James.

2 Answer the questions in the negative form:

a) **Do you love me?**
No, I don't love you.

b) Does she like you?
_____

c) Do you know my father?
_____

d) Do your parents like pop music?
_____

36 thirty-six

3 Make a list of sports you like and you don't like.

> basketball – soccer – swimming – table tennis – running – volleyball
> badminton – horse ridding – skating – skiing – mountain climbing

I like: _____   I don't like: _____
I like: _____   I don't like: _____
I like: _____   I don't like: _____
I like: _____   I don't like: _____

4 What kind of people do you like?

> talkative – sad – angry – nervous – friendly – sweet
> calm – dishonest – mean – violent – kind – honest

I like _____ but I don't like _____
I like _____ but I don't like _____
I like _____ but I don't like _____

REVIEW

1 Follow the pattern:

a) **(fish – chicken)**   **Do you like fish? No, I don't. I prefer chicken.**
b) (soup – salad)   _____
c) (cake – ice cream)   _____

2 Follow the pattern:

a) **(she lives in Brazil – Portugal)**
   Does she live in Brazil? No, she doesn't. She lives in Portugal.
b) (he plays football – tennis)
   _____
c) (the teacher lives in a house – flat)
   _____

3 Change to the negative form:

a) **They go to school.**   **They don't go to school.**
b) We study English.   _____
c) She likes salad.   _____
d) They hate fish.   _____
e) My mother cooks well.   _____
f) He eats chicken.   _____
g) My brother likes potatoes.   _____

4 Look at the pictures and at the model and answer the questions:

Observação: usamos **which** (qual) em vez de **what** (qual) quando temos de escolher uma entre várias coisas.

a) Here are a pear and an apple.

Which do you prefer? (the apple)

I prefer the apple. I don't like pears.

b) Here are two vegetables: cabbage and lettuce.

Which do you prefer? (lettuce)

_____

c) Here are two flowers: a rose and a carnation.

Which do you prefer? (the carnation)

_____

d) Here are two cars: a Mercedes Benz and a Volks.

Which do you prefer? (the Mercedes Benz)

_____

e) Here are two means of transportation: a motorcycle and a horse.

Which do you prefer? (the horse)

_____

f) Here are two blouses: One is red and the other is green.

Which do you prefer? (the green one)

_____

5 Write the possessive adjective according to the subject:

a) I have _____ house.

b) The pupils are sitting on _____ chairs.

c) Where are your parents? _____ parents are at home.

d) Mary is driving _____ car.

e) John is painting _____ house.

f) We sell clothes. _____ clothes are modern and cheap.

g) At midday we come back home for _____ lunch.

6 Answer the questions:

a) **Where is your car? (in the garage)**
   My car is in the garage.

b) Where is your book? (in the drawer)
_____

c) Where is her blouse? (on the bed)
_____

d) Where are his friends? (at the party)
_____

e) Where are their parents? (at home)
_____

7 Answer affirmatively. Follow the pattern:

a) **Do you help your mother?**   Yes, I do. I help my mother.

b) **Does she sweep the house?**   Yes, she does. She sweeps the house.

c) Do you speak English every day?   _____

d) Does she understand Spanish?   _____

e) Do you speak Japanese?   _____

f) Do they study at night?   _____

g) Do you go to school by bus?   _____

FUN TIME

1 Word hunt

Find these words in English:

gostar – casa – gentil – cabelo

X	C	V	X	Z	B	E	R	T	U	O	Q	E	A	X	E	A	D	T	W
N	B	V	C	X	Z	L	K	H	G	B	A	H	A	I	R	G	F	D	A
C	X	Z	D	F	U	R	R	E	A	Q	O	U	Y	R	E	Q	N	B	V
B	V	C	X	Z	B	O	U	Y	T	R	E	Q	K	H	G	F	D	A	U
B	V	C	X	Z	T	R	D	S	A	T	E	O	L	I	K	E	N	B	A
N	B	G	B	R	A	U	O	Y	R	D	S	Q	T	R	X	Z	G	H	P
B	V	C	X	H	O	U	S	E	B	V	C	X	Z	R	T	U	O	E	Q
N	H	G	F	D	A	E	R	T	D	A	U	N	D	C	X	A	U	O	T
V	C	X	Y	T	R	E	Q	H	Z	F	D	S	A	K	I	N	D	U	Y
T	C	V	S	Z	A	E	R	Q	U	O	P	E	A	X	R	A	Q	T	W

thirty-nine **39**

2 Spot the differences

Spot twelve differences between these two pictures:

The prisoner is getting away. The prisoner is getting away.

3 Complete the star crossword in English:

a) homem

b) carro

c) homens

d) novo

e) cama

f) chá

g) todos

h) velho

i) você

j) cachorro

k) dela

l) ver

40 forty

Lesson 6

Genitive Case: Interrogative Pronoun Whose

Lost and Found

Teacher: Whose cap is this?
Jim: It's mine!
Teacher: Take it and don't lose your things.
Whose purse is this?
Annie: This purse belongs to Monica.
It's Monica's. She's absent today.
And this blouse is hers, too.
Teacher: Can you take her things?
Annie: Of course, teacher.
Teacher: Whose schoolbag is this? Does it belong to Mary?
Jason: No, it doesn't. It belongs to James.

TEXT COMPREHENSION

1
a) Where are the lost things?
_____

b) The cap belongs to:
( ) Jason   ( ) Jim   ( ) Annie

c) The teacher asks Jim
( ) not to lose his things   ( ) not to talk in class

d) Complete:
The purse and the blouse belong to _____.

e) Is Monica present or absent from class today?
_____

f) Who takes the purse and the blouse to Monica?
_____

g) Is the schoolbag Mary's?
_____

h) Does it belong to James?
_____

2 Write the sentences under the appropriate pictures:

This is Jim's cap.   This is Monica's blouse.

this purse belongs to Monica.   This schoolbag belongs to James.

a)
_____

b)
_____

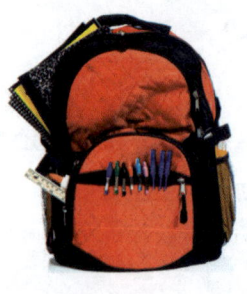

c)
_____

d)
_____

42 forty-two

LEARN THIS

GENITIVE CASE or POSSESSIVE CASE

1. No caso possessivo, o nome do possuidor recebe um apóstrofo e um **s** (**'s**) ou apenas um apóstrofo se terminar por **s**. Observe:

Jessica's (de Jéssica) – **James'** (de James)

(Quando o possuidor for nome de pessoa e terminar por **s**, pode-se, também, usar **'s: James's**)

2. No caso possessivo, há inversão do possuidor e da coisa possuída. Observe:

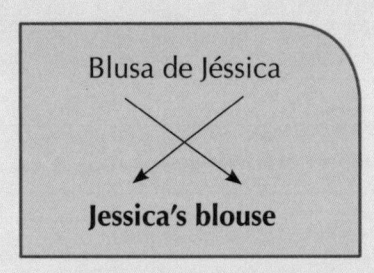

Blusa de Jéssica

Jessica's blouse

Quando há mais de um possuidor da mesma coisa, o **'s** vai no último nomeado.

Ex.: **Jessica, Mary and Jason's house**. (Casa de Jéssica, de Mary e de Jason.)

3. Quando o possuidor não é pessoa, usa-se a preposição **of**:

The pages of the book. (As páginas do livro.)

4. Whose significa de quem. Usa-se para se perguntar quem é o possuidor de algo:

Whose blouse is this? (De quem é esta blusa?)

5. O verbo **to belong** significa pertencer.

This house belongs to Peter. (Esta casa pertence a Peter.)

Does this car belong to Alfred? (Este carro pertence a Alfred?)

ACTIVITIES

1 Follow the pattern. Use is or are:

a) **(car – Peter)**
   Whose car is this? Is it Peter's?
   Yes, it is.

b) **(books – Robert)**
   Whose books are these? Are they Robert's?
   Yes, they are.

c) (blouse – Betty)

d) (watch – Mary)

e) (shoes – Davis)

forty-three **43**

2 Follow the pattern:

a) (Jane – dress)

Jane has a dress. The dress belongs to Jane. It's Jane's dress.

b) (Mary – blouse)

_____

_____

c) (Mario – watch)

_____

_____

d) (Helen – purse)

_____

_____

e) (Charles – bicycle)

_____

_____

3 Write in English:

a) Este carro pertence a Davis.

_____

_____

b) Estes livros pertencem a Charles.

_____

_____

c) De quem é este cinto?

_____

_____

d) De quem são estes sapatos?

_____

_____

Lesson 7

POSSESSIVE ADJECTIVES; POSSESSIVE PRONOUNS; INTERROGATIVE WHOSE

Whose dog is this?

Paul: — Whose dog is this?
George: — It's Natalie's.

At the lost and found animal section

Natalie: George, I am so sad! My dog disappeared! I'm desperate. I must find my dog!
George: Let's go to the lost and Found animal section...
Natalie: Good idea! Let's go!
George: Look at that dog... near the black dog... On the right... It's yours! Call it!
Natalie: Fox! Fox! Come here! Come, Fox! (Fox runs to Natalie. She is very happy and hugs her dog.)
George: It is a happy day. Take your dog and let's go home.

TEXT COMPREHENSION

1 Choose the correct alternative:
( ) Only George's dog disappeared.
( ) Only Natalie's dog disappeared.
( ) Natalie's and George's dogs disappeared.

2 Who's sad and desperate?
_____

3 Why is Natalie sad and desperate?
_____

4 Where does Natalie go to find her dog?
_____

5 Does Natalie find her dog?
_____

6 Does George help Natalie find her dog?
_____

7 What's the name of Natalie's dog?
_____

LEARN THIS
POSSESSIVE ADJECTIVES and POSSESSIVE PRONOUNS

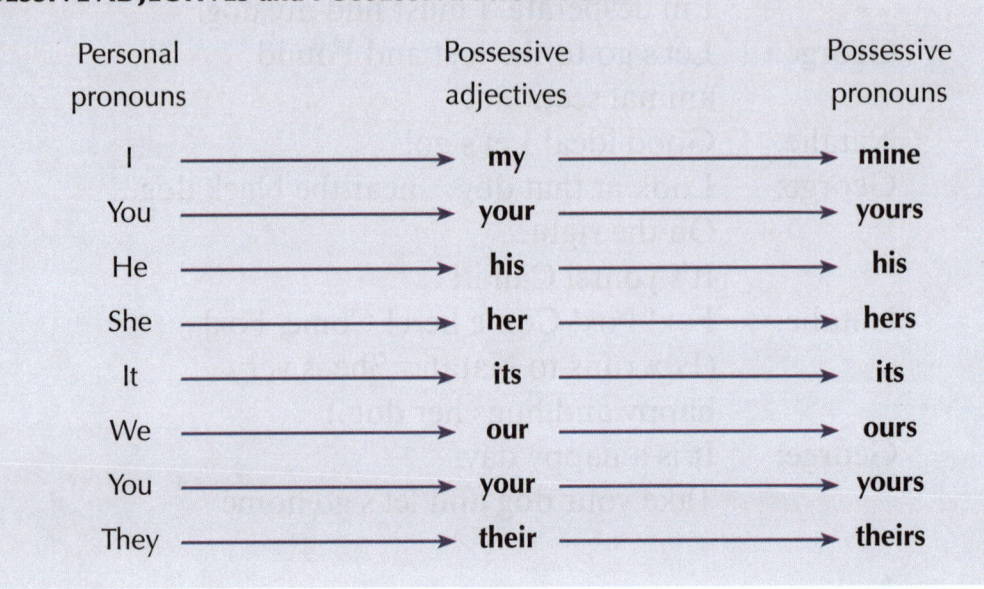

Personal pronouns	Possessive adjectives	Possessive pronouns
I	my	mine
You	your	yours
He	his	his
She	her	hers
It	its	its
We	our	ours
You	your	yours
They	their	theirs

46 forty-six

Observações:

1. Os adjetivos possessivos (**possessive adjectives**) precedem os substantivos:
   My dog is black. (Meu cachorro é preto.)

2. Os pronomes possessivos (**possessive pronouns**) substituem os substantivos:
   My dog is black, yours is white. (Meu cachorro é preto, o seu é branco.)

3. Os pronomes possessivos terminam com a letra **s**, com exceção de **mine**.

ACTIVITIES

1 Follow the pattern:

a) **(house – old)**
   Is that your house?
   No, it is not. Mine is old.

b) (ball – red)

c) (dog – black)

d) (pen – new)

e) (mother – young)

2 Follow the pattern:

a) **(eyes – blue – green)**   My eyes are blue but hers are green.

b) (hair – short – long)

c) (country – large – small)

forty-seven **47**

3 Follow the pattern:

a) (Mike – dog)   The dog belongs to Mike. It's his.

b) (book – John)

_____

c) (house – Mary and John)

_____

4 Translate into English:

Minha casa é velha, mas a dela é nova.

_____

ROLE-PLAY – ORAL DRILL

Whose = de quem?

Ask questions to a classmate using whose and the possessive case.

Aponte para um objeto da classe e pergunte a um(a) colega:

– **Whose... is this? – Whose... is that?**

Veja os exemplos:

a) Você pega um livro e faz a pergunta:

– **Whose book is this?**

Um(a) colega responde de quem é o livro:

– **That book is Maria's (Pedro's, etc.).**

Você mostra uma mochila:

– **Whose schoolbag is this/that?**

Um(a) colega responde de quem é a mochila:

– **That schoolbag is.../It belongs to...**

b) Você pergunta:

– **Is this book Maria's? (Pedro's, Joana's...)**

Um(a) colega responde:

– **Yes, it is Maria's. or – No, it is not. It is Joana's book.**

Lesson 8

MODAL VERB CAN, CANNOT/CAN'T, COULD

We can enjoy life in contact with nature

In contact with nature we can admire beautiful landscapes, smell the perfume of the flowers, hear the birds singing, pick up flowers...

We can also walk, run, jump and rest under a beautiful tree.

TEXT COMPREHENSION

1 Name some activities we can do in contact with nature.
_____
_____

2 Match the columns according to the text:

We can smell	the birds singing.
We can admire	the perfume of flowers.
We can hear	nature.

3 Match the columns according to the text:

Beautiful	a beautiful tree.
Rest under	sing.
The birds	landscapes.

LEARN THIS

1. Modal verb can (poder)
   a) Os verbos modais funcionam como auxiliares do verbo principal. **Modal verb can** expressa permissão, capacidade física ou mental e possibilidade.
   b) Sempre depois do **modal can**, o verbo principal deve vir no infinitivo sem o "**to**".
   Exemplo: **She can speak French very well**. (Ela pode falar francês muito bem.)
   c) O **modal can** não sofre alteração na terceira pessoa do singular no presente, isto é, nunca recebe "**s**", "**es**" ou "**ies**".
   Expressando capacidade:
   I can sing and dance. (Eu posso cantar e dançar.)
   The athlete can jump two meters high. (O atleta pode pular dois metros de altura.)
   Expressando permissão:
   We can study in the library. (Podemos estudar na biblioteca.)
   d) O verbo **can** possui duas formas negativas **cannot** e **can't**.
   Exemplo: **You can't drive your father's car**. (Você não pode dirigir o carro do seu pai.)
   You cannot drive your father's car.

Modal verb can (simple present tense)		
Affirmative form	**Negative form**	**Contracted form**
I can	I cannot	I can't
You can	You cannot	You can't
He can	He cannot	He can't
She can	She cannot	She can't
It can	It cannot	It can't
We can	We cannot	We can't
You can	You cannot	You can't
They can	They cannot	They can't

> **Observações**
>
> Verbo **can** é utilizado na interrogativa para expressar permissão:
> **Can I go now?** (Posso ir agora?)
> **Can I come in?** (Posso entrar?)

e) Os verbos **can** e **may** são empregados para denotar permissão, licença, com a diferença que **may** é mais formal.
Exemplos: **Can I go to the bathroom?** (Posso ir ao banheiro?)
May I come in, Mr. Johnson? (Posso entrar, Mr. Johnson?)

f) A forma do verbo **can** no passado é **could** (podia).

| Modal verb can (past tense) ||
Affirmative form	Tradução
I could	Eu podia, pude
You could	Você podia, pôde
He could	Ele podia, pôde
She could	Ela podia, pôde
It could	Ele/ela podia, pôde
We could	Nós podíamos, pudemos
You could	Vocês podiam, puderam
They could	Eles, elas podiam, puderam

Exemplos: **I could sing and dance when I was a teenager.**
Helen could speak English very well.

g) **Could** também serve para expressar:
  1) Possibilidade: **Tom could come to my party**. (Tom podia vir a minha festa.)
  2) Solicitação formal: **Could you tell me the time?** (Poderia me dizer as horas?)

ACTIVITIES

1 Complete the sentences with these expressions:

> a picture – a story – a flower – a car – the door – my friends – a text to school – a book – English – fresh water – your mother

I can...

a) invite _____
b) smell _____
c) drive _____
d) speak _____
e) read _____
f) write _____
g) tell _____
h) go _____
i) paint _____
j) close _____
k) drink _____
l) help _____

fifty-one **51**

REVIEW

1 Substitute the underlined words by the possessive pronouns:

a) That house is her house.
That house is hers.

b) Those magazines are <u>my magazines</u>.
_____

c) That purse is <u>her purse</u>.
_____

d) Is this dog <u>his dog</u>?
_____

e) Is that ball <u>your ball</u>?
_____

f) No, it's not <u>my ball</u>. It's Bob's.
_____

g) Is that table <u>our table</u>?
_____

h) This wallet is not <u>my wallet</u>.
_____

i) This book is not yours. <u>Your book</u> is old.
_____

2 Follow the pattern:

a) Whose car is this? (Peter)
This car belongs to Peter.
It's his car.

b) Whose house is this? (Mark)
_____
_____

c) Whose purse is that? (Mary)
_____

d) Whose farm is that? (John)
_____
_____

e) Whose picture is that? (my mother)
_____
_____

3 Follow the pattern:

a) My trousers are blue. Your trousers are black.
My trousers are blue but yours are black.

b) My parents are old. Your parents are young.
_____

c) My dog is black. Her dog is brown.
_____

4 Answer the questions:

a) My father is young, and yours? (old)
Mine is old.

b) My eyes are brown, and hers? (blue)
_____

c) Our car is yellow, and his? (red)
_____

d) My father is tall, and yours? (short)
_____

5 Change to English using the genitive case:

a) **a casa de Peter**
   Peter's house

b) o carro do professor
   _____

c) a bicicleta de Nelson
   _____

d) a bola de Luís.
   _____

6 Insert the apostrophe in the correct place:

a) I'm going to buy the childrens toys.
b) Mr Nelsons car is black.
c) My sisters bedroom is clean.
d) She goes to the dentists on Saturdays.

7 Answer the questions using the shortened possessive form:

> **Observações**
>
> Na forma possessiva abreviada dispensamos o uso das palavras **office** (escritório, consultório), **shop** (loja), **house** (casa) etc.

a) **Where are you going? (John's house)**
   I'm going to John's.

b) Where is she going? (doctor's office)
   _____

c) Where are you going? (dentist's office)
   _____

8 Follow the pattern:

a) **(car – belongs – Mary)**
   The car belongs to Mary.

b) (book – belongs – the teacher)
   _____

c) (watch – belongs – John)
   _____

9 Write his, her, its, their according to the pictures:

a) _____ ball is red.

b) _____ dog is big.

c) The girl likes _____ doll.

d) _____ tail is very long.

10 Change to the negative form:

a) **I can lift the table.**

   I cannot lift the table.

   I can't lift the table.

b) I can see well.

c) I can buy the present for you.

d) We can understand you.

11 Ask polite questions using verb could:

a) **(tell me the time)**

   Could you tell me the time?

b) (show me the way to school)

c) (tell me where the drugstore is)

FUN TIME

1 Vocabulary ladder

a)
b)
c)
d)
e)
f)
g)

54 fifty-four

Lesson 9

MODAL VERBS: NEED TO/HAVE TO/MUST

I must, you must...

You must go to school! Without education there is no future.

Take these clothes. They're yours. You must take a bath and change your clothes. They are too dirty. In the next square there is a public bathroom.

I have to go now, otherwise I miss the bus. Bye!

I need to study for my exams.

TEXT COMPREHENSION

1 Why must people go to school?

Because without _____

2 There is a good woman in the text. What does she give to a poor man in the street?

_____

3 The poor man's clothes are

( ) clean   ( ) dirty

4 Complete:

The woman asks the poor man to _____ a _____ and change his _____.

5 What is the meaning of the expression "do not disturb"?

_____

6 Why must the girl in the text go now?

Because he can miss _____.

LEARN THIS

MODAL VERBS: **Must**   **Have to**   **Need to**
                (dever, precisar)   (ter de)   (precisar)

1. Esses verbos são usados para expressar obrigação ou necessidade:

I must study English. (Preciso estudar inglês.)

I have to go to the bank. (Tenho de ir ao banco.)

I need to take my medicine. (Preciso tomar meu remédio.)

2. Must não tem uma forma para o passado. Na ausência dessa forma usamos **had to**:

I must go to school. (Preciso ir à escola.)

I had to go to school. (Eu tinha de ir à escola.)

3. A forma negativa desses verbos é feita colocando-se **not** depois deles:

You mustn't go now. (Você não deve ir agora.)

You haven't to go now. (Você não precisa ir agora.)

You needn't go now. (Você não precisa ir agora.)

4. O verbo **need** pode funcionar como um verbo comum:

Do you need some money? (Você precisa de algum dinheiro?)

5. Mustn't indica proibição: **You mustn't talk to the driver.** (Você não deve conversar com o motorista).

56 fifty-six

ACTIVITIES

1 Follow the pattern:
   a) **My teeth are very bad. (go to the dentist's)**   **I must go to the dentist's.**
   b) I have no money. (go to the bank) _____
   c) I am hungry. (eat something) _____
   d) I am thirsty. (drink some water) _____
   e) I am cold. (put on my coat) _____
   f) I am going to eat. (wash my hands) _____
   g) I am going to sleep. (brush my teeth) _____

2 Follow the pattern:
   a) **(study your lessons)**   **Don't forget: you must study your lessons.**
   b) (go to the dentist's) _____
   c) (water the flowers) _____
   d) (read the book) _____
   e) (sign the documents) _____

3 Follow the pattern:
   a) **(talk aloud – in the cinema)**   **You mustn't talk aloud in the cinema.**
   b) (talk to the driver – on the bus) _____
   c) (pick up flowers – in the park) _____
   d) (feed the animals – in the zoo) _____
   e) (touch the fruit – at the market) _____
   f) (smoke – near the children) _____

4 Follow the pattern:
   a) **You must cut the grass.**   **You had to cut the grass.**
   b) She must attend school. _____
   c) They must read the book. _____
   d) We must pay the bill. _____
   e) I must work hard. _____
   f) He must find a job. _____

fifty-seven **57**

Lesson 10
Past tense of regular verbs

Old times × modern times

When I was young, life was very different from today.

In old times men generally worked hard in the field and raised domestic animals, as pigs, cows, hens, goats, or planted vegetables, wheat, corn, tomatoes, potatoes... But today most families prefer to live in large cities where they can find more comfort, health protection, drugstores, schools, shops, amusement, supermarkets, shopping malls...

In old times people had a healthy life because they lived directly in contact with nature but today they live in large polluted cities.

In old times costumes were different from today. For example: women preferred to wear long dresses and stayed at home most of the time, but today they wear modern clothes and have many opportunities to get good jobs in the city.

TEXT COMPREHENSION

Answer according to the text:

1. What's the opposite of modern times? _____

2. Is life today different from life in old times? _____

3. Complete:

   In old times men generally worked in the field and raised _____

   or planted _____

4. Where do most families prefer to live today? _____

5. Why do most families prefer to live in large cities?

   Because in large cities they can find _____

6. Write the part of the text that refers to each picture below:

In old times.
_____
_____

In modern times.
_____
_____

7. Do you have a photo or a picture of old times? If you have it show it to your classmates.

LEARN THIS

PAST TENSE

I lived → (eu vivi ou vivia)		**We lived** → (nós vivemos ou vivíamos)
You lived → (você viveu ou vivia)		**You lived** → (vocês viveram ou viviam)
He/she/it lived → (ele/ela viveu ou vivia)		**They lived** → (eles/elas viveram ou viviam)

1. Os verbos regulares no passado terminam por **ed** e têm a mesma forma para todas as pessoas.

   Exemplos: work   live   pull   dance
              worked lived   pulled danced

fifty-nine 59

2. Os verbos irregulares têm no pretérito diferentes formas verbais:
   to go (ir)   **went** (foi)   **to find** (encontrar)   **found** (encontrou)

3. Os verbos terminados em **y** precedido de vogal recebem **ed** no pretérito. Quando o **y** for precedido de consoante, muda-se o **y** por **i** e acrescenta-se **ed**:
   play – played   **obey – obeyed**   **study – studied**   **copy – copied**

ACTIVITIES

1 Write (**R**) for regular verbs and (**I**) for irregular verbs:

a) to work – worked ( ) (trabalhar – trabalhou)

b) to see – saw ( ) (ver – viu)

c) to live – lived ( ) (morar – morou)

d) to stay – stayed ( ) (ficar – ficou)

e) to have – had ( ) (ter – teve)

f) to use – used ( ) (usar – usou)

2 Write in the past tense:

a) I work hard in the country.   I worked hard in the country.

b) I live in a city.   _____

c) They stay home all the time.   _____

d) She likes to wear modern clothes.   _____

e) Women like to stay at home.   _____

f) We love our parents.   _____

g) She wants to see the film.   _____

3 Change to the past tense:

a) I study in the morning.   I studied in the morning.

b) I try to understand you.   _____

c) Men carry the bags.   _____

d) The baby cries because he is hungry.   _____

e) The teacher simplifies the test.   _____

f) He marries his daughter to a dentist.   _____

Lesson 11
Past tense of regular and irregular verbs

Saint Peter's farm

This is the farm where Paul lived when he was young.
There they raised animals and planted vegetables.
They also had a large orchard with fruit trees.

Some years ago ... and ... today.

Paul lived on a big farm named Saint Peter...

But now he lives in a big city.

When he was a little boy, Paul used to go to school on foot...

But now he drives his own car.

When he was a little boy, Paul studied at a small school named Teacher Rose...

But now he studies Biology at a big university.

When he was a little boy, Paul worked on a farm named Saint Peter.

Now he works in a big medicine laboratory.

TEXT COMPREHENSION

Answer according to the text:

1 What's the name of the farm where Paul lived?
_____

2 What was the name of Paul's school?
_____

3 Paul used to go to school:

( ) by car   ( ) on foot

4 Where does he live today?
_____

5 Where does he study today?
_____

6 What is he studying at the university?
_____

7 Today Paul goes to the university:

( ) on foot   ( ) by his own car

8 Where is he working now?
_____

LEARN THIS

REGULAR VERBS

Observe:

Infinitive – Past
to work – worked (trabalhou, trabalhava);
to live – lived (morou, morava).
Forma-se o passado dos verbos regulares acrescentando-se **ed** ou **d** ao infinitivo.

Infinitive – Past
to study – studied (estudou, estudava)
Quando o verbo terminar em **y**, precedido de consoante, muda-se o **y** por **i** e acrescenta-se **ed**.

PAST TENSE

To work
I worked (eu trabalhei, trabalhava)
You worked
He worked
She worked
We worked
You worked
They worked

Irregular verbs

Verbos irregulares são aqueles que não têm o passado terminado em **ed**.
Observe:
Infinitive – Past
to speak – spoke (falou, falava);
to find – found (encontrou, encontrava).
They found the data on the Internet.

Infinitive	Past tense
to find	found
	I found (eu achei, achava)
	You found
	He found
	She found
	We found
	You found
	They found

Observações

O **past tense** é utilizado quando queremos expressar uma ação finalizada. Geralmente é utilizado junto com uma expressão de tempo:
I lived in Rio in 1985. (Eu morei no Rio em 1985.)
We visited Cristina yesterday. (Visitamos a Cristina ontem.)

ACTIVITIES

1 Fill in the blanks with the following words.

> studies   lives   own   lived   was

a) When I _____ a little boy, I _____ on a farm.
b) Now, he drives his _____ car.
c) Now, he _____ in a city.
d) He _____ at a small school.

2 Write (**R**) for regular verbs and (**I**) for irregular verbs:

Infinitive	Past tense		
a) to live	lived	(R)	(morou...)
b) to work	worked	( )	(trabalhou...)
c) to take	took	( )	(pegou...)
d) to sleep	slept	( )	(dormiu...)
e) to see	saw	( )	(viu...)
f) to play	played	( )	(jogou...)
g) to study	studied	( )	(estudou...)
h) to look	looked	( )	(olhou...)

sixty-five **65**

3 Write the past tense of these regular verbs:

infinitive	Past Tense	
to answer	answered	(respondeu...)
to call		(chamou...)
to cross		(cruzou...)
to dance		(dançou...)
to paint		(pintou...)
to rest		(descansou...)

Some very used irregular verbs:
Learn these irregular verbs in the past tense form:

to be – WAS – WERE
(ser, estar)

to have – HAD
(ter)

to drink – DRANK
(beber)

to take – TOOK
(pegar, levar)

to speak – SPOKE
(falar)

to go – WENT
(ir)

to get up – GOT UP
(levantar)

to find – FOUND
(encontrar)

to see – SAW
(ver)

to come – CAME
(vir)

4 Complete the sentences using the past tense of the verbs in parenthesis:

a) I _____ Mary yesterday. (to see)

b) Paul and Mary _____ to school in the morning. (to go)

c) They _____ back at 1 o'clock. (to come)

d) My mother _____ at 6 o'clock. (to get up)

e) I _____ breakfast at 7 o'clock. (to have)

f) She _____ to me in English. (to speak)

g) I _____ a glass of milk. (to drink)

h) They _____ in the library. (to be)

i) She _____ at home. (to be)

j) They _____ the books from the shelf. (to take)

5 Write the opposites of the words below. Use the opposites in the box:

> obey – winter – dirty – hot – can't – night – old – bad

clean	_____	good	_____
day	_____	can	_____
summer	_____	new	_____
disobey	_____	cold	_____

FUN TIME

1 Complete the crossword with verbs in the present tense and in the past tense:

Past and present tense crossword puzzle

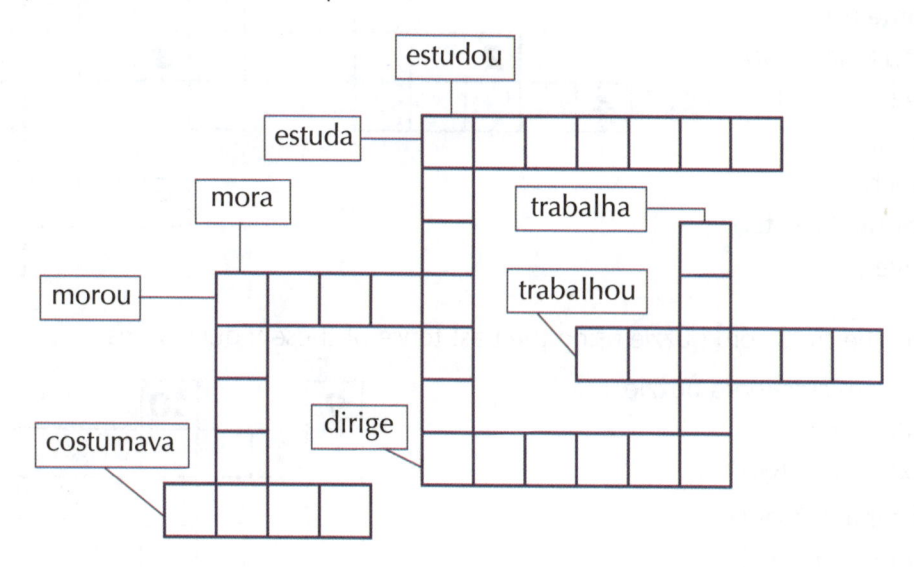

estudou
estuda
mora   trabalha
morou   trabalhou
costumava dirige

2 Connect the sentences according to the meaning:

- Paul lives on a farm.
- Paul lived on a farm.
- He used to walk to school.
- He works on a big farm.
- He worked on a big farm.
- He studies at a university.

- Ele costumava ir a pé para a escola.
- Ele trabalha numa grande fazenda.
- Paul mora numa fazenda.
- Paul morou numa fazenda.
- Ele trabalhou numa grande fazenda.
- Ele estuda numa universidade.

sixty-seven 67

3 Find these words

industry   farm   own   city   walks   studied

```
W A O D M N S K S L S K J F U R E C I T Y P Q A L X Z M J K U I
T Y S M E N R I T O K D J S H J S T U D I E D W I K K S W N M A
M C O O W N Q W E R T Y U F A R M P L K I O J H Y U G F T R D S
D I E D M J K I U S E D R D S M I N D U S T R Y Q W E R T Y T R
N J U H Y G T F R D E S W W A L K S P O L K I J U H U Y G Y F T
```

4 Complete the crossword puzzle using the past tense of these irregular verbs:

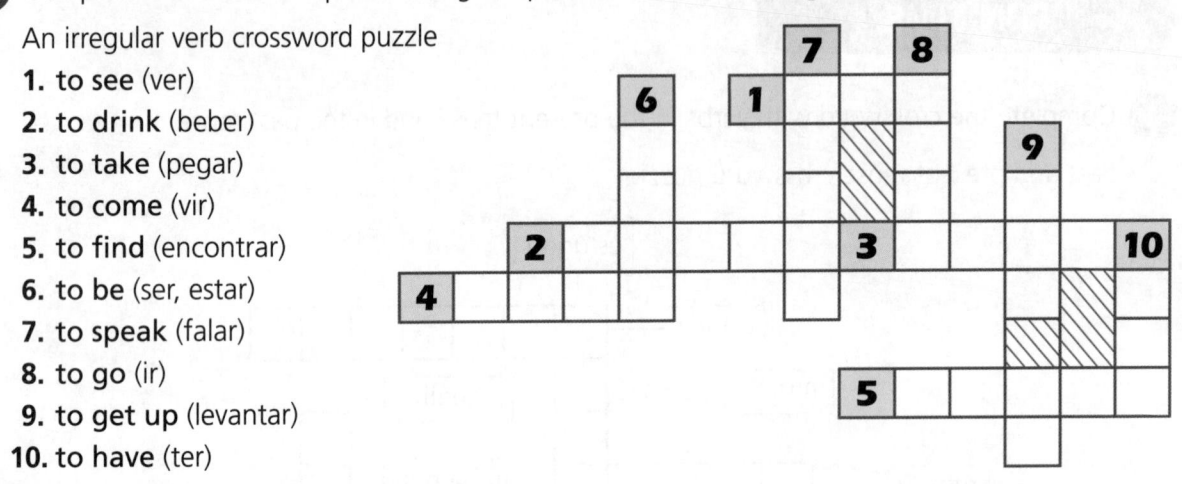

An irregular verb crossword puzzle

1. to see (ver)
2. to drink (beber)
3. to take (pegar)
4. to come (vir)
5. to find (encontrar)
6. to be (ser, estar)
7. to speak (falar)
8. to go (ir)
9. to get up (levantar)
10. to have (ter)

5 Complete the crossword puzzle using the past tense of these regular verbs.

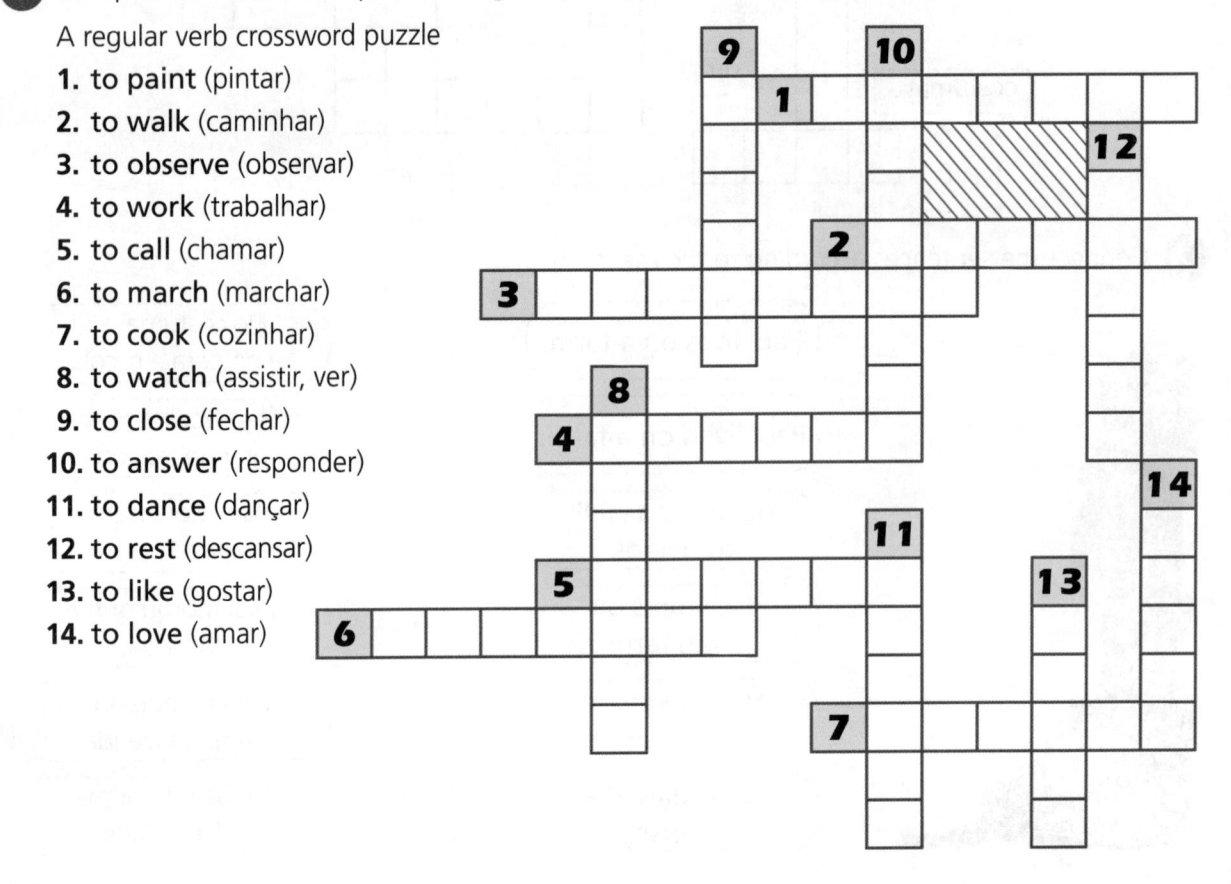

A regular verb crossword puzzle

1. to paint (pintar)
2. to walk (caminhar)
3. to observe (observar)
4. to work (trabalhar)
5. to call (chamar)
6. to march (marchar)
7. to cook (cozinhar)
8. to watch (assistir, ver)
9. to close (fechar)
10. to answer (responder)
11. to dance (dançar)
12. to rest (descansar)
13. to like (gostar)
14. to love (amar)

68 sixty-eight

John's daily routine

6 Write these sentences in the past tense according to the pictures:
- John gets up at 7.
- He has a shower.
- and then he has breakfast.
- He starts to work at 8 and
- has lunch at 1.
- He comes back home at 7.
- In the evening he watches TV.
- He goes to bed at 10.

a) Yesterday John _____

b) _____

c) _____

d) _____

e) _____

f) _____

g) _____

h) _____

sixty-nine **69**

LISTEN AND WRITE – DICTATION

_____ is the _____ where Peter _____.

He _____ to walk to _____.

He was a _____.

_____, he works at a big laboratory.

FUN TIME

7 Word hunt

Find the past of these verbs on the sheep:

live – clean – open – brush –
play – carry – obey – try – use

I am not a ship!
I am a sheep!

```
    H S E B
  S H O C K S
 Y H W D H K O P E N E D T R E A
 T S P L A Y E D S H Z H T R I H S
 S U B P M E O T S U S E D A I A S O
 L C H O B E Y E D E L V P L D H N E R H
 O K S H O T L L T T B R U S H E D
 R O L I V E D S E R N P E W S E T
 D T D W T R I E D H I E H O O H
   U C B E M A H C L E A N E D
     C A R R I E D K S S P
         B       S S I H
       K         H E O
                   W
```

8 Write the past tense of these verbs:
a) discover
b) disobey
c) finish
d) escape
e) wait
f) like
g) use

70 seventy

Lesson 12

Past tense of regular verbs: interrogative and negative forms

Did you buy some dessert?

My father worked hard until 6 o'clock p.m. Then my mother called him:

– John, did you buy some cheese for dinner?

– Yes, I did.

– And did you buy some dessert?

– No, I didn't, but I'm going to buy it just now.

And when he arrived my mother kissed him and they talked for some minutes.

Then my mother cooked a meal and prepared a nice salad. My father likes salad and fruit very much. After dinner they washed the dishes and watched a long film on TV.

TEXT COMPREHENSION

Answer according to the text:

a) Who worked hard until 6 p.m.?
_____

b) Who called Luciene's father?
_____

c) Did Luciene's father buy some cheese for dinner?
_____

d) Did Luciene's father cook the meal?
_____

e) Who cooked dinner?
_____

f) Does John like salad and fruit?
_____

g) What did they do after dinner?
_____
_____

LEARN THIS

Regular verbs (past tense)

Interrogative form

Observe os exemplos:

She kissed my father. (Ela beijou meu pai.)
Did she kiss my father? (Ela beijou meu pai?)
They arrived late. (Eles chegaram tarde.)
Did they arrive late? (Eles chegaram tarde?)

Para se obter a forma interrogativa com verbos comuns, usamos **do** ou **does** para o presente e **did** para o passado, tendo, porém, o cuidado de deixar o verbo principal na forma básica. Obtém-se a forma básica suprimindo-se o **ed** ou **d** do tempo passado. Observe:

Passado:	**washed**	**worked**	**arrived**
Forma básica:	**wash**	**work**	**arrive**

Negative form (past tense)

Observe os exemplos:

They washed the dishes. (Eles lavaram os pratos.)
They did not wash the dishes. (Eles não lavaram os pratos.)
They didn't wash the dishes. (Eles não lavaram os pratos.)
He liked the salad. (Ele gostou da salada.)
He did not like the salad. (Ele não gostou da salada.)
He didn't like the salad. (Ele não gostou da salada.)

A forma negativa consiste em antepor ao verbo **do not/does not** ou **don't/doesn't** para o presente do indicativo e **did not/didn't** para o passado. Ao receber a negação, o verbo principal perde o **ed** ou **d** característicos do tempo passado.

ACTIVITIES

1 Answer the questions about the text. Follow the pattern:

a) **Did the father work hard?**   Yes, he did. He worked hard.

b) Did he call my mother? _____

c) Did my mother kiss my father? _____

d) Did they talk for some minutes? _____

e) Did my mother cook a meal? _____

f) Did she prepare a nice salad? _____

2 Change to the interrogative form:

a) **John worked hard yesterday.**
   Did John work hard yesterday?

b) He arrived on time.

_____

c) He returned home by bus.

_____

d) She prepared a nice salad.

_____

e) You washed the dishes.

_____

3 Change to the negative form:

a) **They worked hard.**
   They did not work hard. They didn't work hard.

b) I liked the film.

_____

c) We invited John.

_____

d) She washed the dishes.

_____

seventy-three **73**

Lesson 13

PAST TENSE OF IRREGULAR VERBS

Reasons for a long life

Mr Benson became a very remarkable person in the remote village of Greenfield. The reason: he is one hundred years old.

Last month a reporter came to the village and asked Mr Benson the secret of his long life:

– Do you have a secret for a long life?

Here is what Mr Benson said:

– I have no secrets, but I have some rules for a long life. First thing: you mustn't give up all the pleasures of life. Second thing: you may enjoy the pleasures of life moderately. For example, I drink one glass of yoghurt in my breakfast. The third thing is to walk and do some exercise every day.

TEXT COMPREHENSION

1. Did Mr Benson become an important person in his village?

2. Where is Mr Benson from?

3. How old is Mr Benson?

4. Who interviews Mr Benson?

5. What question did the reporter ask to Mr Benson?

6. In your opinion, what's the best rule for a long life?

LEARN THIS

IRREGULAR VERBS

Infinitive	Past tense	Past participle
to go (ir)	**went** (foi)	**gone** (ido)
to give (dar)	**gave** (deu)	**given** (dado)

Verbos irregulares são aqueles que não terminam por **ed** no passado. Por serem de uso muito frequente, torna-se necessário aprendê-los por meio de exercícios repetidos ou decorá-los.
A lista dos verbos irregulares está no fim do livro.
Veja alguns:

	Infinitive	Past tense	Past participle	Translation
1.	to come	came	come	vir
2.	to become	became	become	tornar-se
3.	to begin	began	begun	começar
4.	to buy	bought	bought	comprar
5.	to drink	drank	drunk	beber
6.	to eat	ate	eaten	comer
7.	to find	found	found	achar, encontrar
8.	to meet	met	met	encontrar (pessoas)
9.	to know	knew	known	conhecer, saber
10.	to say	said	said	dizer

ACTIVITIES

1 Change into the past tense:

a) **He comes from Portugal.**   He came from Portugal.

b) He becomes a doctor in 1980. _____

c) He begins to study at 8 o'clock. _____

d) They come from France. _____

e) John buys an old piano. _____

f) Bob drinks a lot of water. _____

g) I eat a sandwich. _____

h) She finds some difficulties. _____

i) You know her name. _____

j) I meet my friends at school. _____

2 Change from the past tense to the present tense:

a) **Mr Benson became a remarkable person.**   Mr Benson becomes a remarkable person.

b) A reporter came to the village. _____

c) Mr Benson said: "I have no secrets". _____

d) I knew some important men. _____

e) I drank one glass of yoghurt. _____

3 Esta página está reservada para você inventar frases com verbos irregulares no tempo passado. É fácil. Você pode utilizar as mesmas frases dos exercícios 1 e 2, modificando lugares, profissões, datas, comidas, bebidas, coisas...

Exemplo: letra a do exercício 1:

He came from Portugal.   **You came from Porto Alegre.**
They came from Maceió.   **My parents came from the church.**
She came from Paris.

_____
_____
_____
_____
_____
_____
_____

Lesson 4

PAST TENSE: INTERROGATIVE FORM, IRREGULAR VERBS

The tower with the Big Ben in London

Did you have a nice vacation?

Sandra: Did you have a good vacation, Meg?

Meg: Oh, yes, I had a wonderful time. And you?

Sandra: I went to the South. I met Silvia in Curitiba and we took a bus to Porto Alegre. What a fun time!

Meg: And I went to England. I spoke English with my keypal and he understood me!

Sandra: What did you see in London?

Meg: Oh, I saw so many things! I saw museums, parks, churches, I saw the House of Parliament, Westminster Abbey, London Tower, Trafalgar Square, and so on. And you, Loren, what did you do?

Loren: I went to the beach and stayed at home. I read, wrote some letters, ate, and slept.

Meg: You had a good time too!

TEXT COMPREHENSION

1 a) What are the girls talking about?
___
___

b) Where did Sandra spend her vacation?
___
___

c) Where did Meg go to?
___
___

d) Where did Loren go to?
___
___

e) Sandra and Silvia went to the South

( ) by car   ( ) by bus   ( ) by train   ( ) by airplane

f) According to Meg, did Loren have a good time?
___
___

2 Write Meg or Sandra according to the actions of the text:

(_____) I went to the South.

(_____) I saw museums, parks, and churches.

(_____) I had a wonderful time.

(_____) I saw London Tower and Trafalgar Square.

(_____) I met Silvia in Curitiba.

(_____) I took a bus to Porto Alegre.

(_____) I saw the House of Parliament and Westminster Abbey.

(_____) I went to England.

(_____) I spoke English with my keypal.

(_____) My keypal understood me.

(_____) I traveled by bus.

LEARN THIS

IRREGULAR VERBS – PAST TENSE – INTERROGATIVE FORM

Esquema da forma interrogativa com verbos não auxiliares

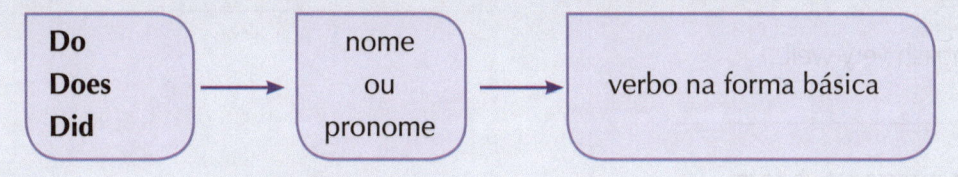

Do / Does / Did → nome ou pronome → verbo na forma básica

Do they go? (Eles vão?)
Does Mary understand? (Mary compreende?)
Did you speak? (Você falou?)

Para se obter a forma interrogativa com verbos irregulares e regulares, usamos **do** ou **does** para o presente e **did** para o passado, tendo, porém, o cuidado de deixar o verbo principal na sua forma básica. (Obtém-se a forma básica suprimindo-se a partícula **to** do infinitivo. Exemplo: **to go**: ir – forma básica: **go**.)

VERBOS IRREGULARES

É importante que você aprenda os verbos irregulares nas suas três formas: infinitivo, passado e particípio passado, sem o que se torna impossível falar inglês.

	Infinitive	Past tense	Past participle	Translation
1.	to have	had	had	ter
2.	to go	went	gone	ir
3.	to take	took	taken	pegar, levar
4.	to speak	spoke	spoken	falar
5.	to understand	understood	understood	compreender
6.	to see	saw	seen	ver
7.	to read	read	read	ler
8.	to write	wrote	written	escrever
9.	to sleep	slept	slept	dormir
10.	to say	said	said	dizer

ACTIVITIES

1 Change into the past tense:

a) I have some friends.
   I had some friends.

b) She goes to school.
   _____

c) I meet my friends at school.
_____

d) I take a bus to go to school.
_____

e) He speaks English very well.
_____

f) They understand me.
_____

g) I read the newspaper in the morning.
_____

2 Change into the interrogative form:

a) **You spoke to Mr Nelson.**
   Did you speak to Mr Nelson?

b) **She went to the bank.**
   _____

c) **The mouse ate all the cheese.**
   _____

d) **He met his friends at the party.**
   _____

3 Answer the questions:

a) **Did you have a good vacation?**
   Yes, I did. I had a good vacation.

b) Did you go to England?
   _____

c) Did you meet Silvia?
   _____

d) Did she write the letters?
   _____

e) Did they eat in a restaurant?
   _____

4 Treine verbos irregulares, forma interrogativa – tempo passado, criando você mesmo frases. É fácil. Basta substituir o termo destacado por outro. Veja o exemplo:

a) **She went to the bank. Did she go to the bank?**
   Did she go to the club? Did she go to the park? Did she go to the drugstore?

b) Liz ate all the sandwiches. Did Liz eat all the **sandwiches**?
   _____

c) They took all the things. Did they take all the **things**?
   _____

d) They read the book. Did they read the **book**?
   _____

e) They spoke to Mr Lee. Did they speak to **Mr Lee**?
   _____

f) Chris saw you at the club. Did Chris see **you** at the club?
   _____

FUN TIME

1 How many animals did Adam have on the ark?

None. Adam didn't go on the ark – Noah did.

2 Missing vowels

Complete the words writing the missing vowels:

a) Sh wnt t th prk. _____

b) Th grl knw th lssn. _____

c) Jhn plyd tnns ystrdy. _____

3 Spot the differences

Find out nine differences between the pictures:

4 At the Post Office

eighty-one **81**

5 Write the past tense of these verbs:

a) say
b) eat
c) come
d) take
e) read
f) begin
g) write
h) have
i) meet
j) buy
k) become
l) give
m) know
n) sleep
o) break
p) go
q) drink

REVIEW

1 Change into the interrogative form:

a) **The children liked the clown.** Did the children like the clown?

b) They decided to go to the party. _____

c) She arrived at six o'clock. _____

d) The children played tennis yesterday. _____

e) John borrowed a lot of money from the bank. _____

2 Change into the negative form:

a) **She waited for me.** She didn't wait for me. (She did not wait for me.)

b) We talked to Peter. _____

c) The teacher explained the lesson. _____

d) The dog barked last night. _____

3 Change into the interrogative form:

a) **John came to class late.** Did John come to class late?

b) They knew my teacher. _____

c) They went to school. _____

d) They bought a new car last week. _____

82 eighty-two

Lesson 15

Past tense; negative form; irregular verbs

At the Police Station

Chief of Police: Is this watch yours?
Boy: Yes, it is mine.
Chief of Police: Do you know its make?
Boy: No, I don't.
Chief of Police: Where did you buy it?
Boy: I didn't buy it.
Chief of Police: Did you receive it as a present?
Boy: No, I didn't.
Chief of Police: Then you stole the watch! Confess!
Boy: No, I didn't. I didn't steal the watch!

I found it near my house.

TEXT COMPREHENSION

1 Answer according to the text:

a) Where's the boy?
___

b) What did the chief of police ask the boy about the make of the watch?
___

c) What did the boy answer?
___

d) Did the boy buy the watch?
___

e) Did the boy receive the watch as a present?
___

f) How many times did the boy answer negatively the questions
___

g) In your opinion, did the boy steal the watch?

( ) Yes he did.   ( ) No, he didn't   ( ) I think he found the watch.

LEARN THIS

BANK OF IRREGULAR VERBS

Infinitive	Past tense	Past participle	Translation
to know	knew	known	saber, conhecer
to buy	bought	bought	comprar
to steal	stole	stolen	roubar
to find	found	found	encontrar
to sell	sold	sold	vender
to pay	paid	paid	pagar
to spend	spent	spent	gastar
to send	sent	sent	enviar
to tell	told	told	contar, dizer
to sit	sat	sat	sentar

ACTIVITIES

1 Change the sentences to the negative form:

a) **He knows many countries.**
   He doesn't know many countries.
   He didn't know many countries.

b) **They buy and sell cars.**
   They don't buy and sell cars.
   They didn't buy and sell cars.

c) He pays the bill.
   _____
   _____

d) That thief steal people's cell phones.
   _____
   _____

e) She understand the text.
   _____
   _____

2 Create sentences in the past tense modifying the first and the last words of the sentences:

a) **They bought and sold cars.**
   She bought and sold computers. Jim bought and sold watches.
   My mother bought and sold clothes.

b) He paid the bill.
   _____

c) That thief stole my hens.
   _____

d) They understood the text.
   _____

e) I sent a telegram.
   _____

f) We sat in front of you.
   _____

Lesson 16

Irregular Verbs: Past Tense Interrogative and Negative Form

Catch the thief!

What did he steal?
He stole my watch, my diamond ring, my purse... my money...
Did you steal her watch?
Look! My watch!
No, I didn't!
He's a thief!
He's a liar!
Did you take her purse?
No, I did not take her purse.
Thief!
Look! My purse!
Liar!
What did he do?
He stole my purse, my money...
Follow me!

TEXT COMPREHENSION

1 Write the words under the appropriate pictures:

> running – thief – watch – ring – purse – money

_____   _____   _____

_____   _____   _____

2 Complete the sentences using the words: **watch**, **thief**, **money**, **ring**:

a) A person who steals is a _____.

b) A round object we wear on a finger. It is generally made of gold or silver. It is a _____.

c) A _____ is a small clock that we wear on our wrist or carry in our pocket.

d) Coins or banknotes that we use to buy or pay things are _____.

3 a) Who is crying for help according to the text?

_____

b) Why is the woman crying for help?
   She is crying for help:
   ( ) because she is not well.
   ( ) because a thief stole her purse, her watch and her ring.

c) Were the people near the robbed woman indifferent to her problem or did they help her to catch the thief?

_____

d) The thief in the text is:
   ( ) a liar   ( ) a sincere person

e) What did the thief take from the woman?

_____

f) The thief carried the woman's objects
   ( ) in his pocket   ( ) in a suitcase   ( ) in a sack

g) Did the thief tell the truth?

_____

88   eighty-eight

LEARN THIS

Past tense ─┬─ Interrogative form
            └─ Negative form

Forma interrogativa no passado

Observe os exemplos:

Mary worked yesterday.
(Mary trabalhou ontem.)

Did Mary work yesterday?
(Mary trabalhou ontem?)

He stole my purse.
(Ele roubou minha bolsa.)

Did he steal my purse?
(Ele roubou minha bolsa?)

Para se perguntar, em inglês, com verbos no passado não auxiliares, usamos o auxiliar **did**. Neste caso, o auxiliar **did** não tem tradução. É simplesmente um indicador de que a pergunta está sendo feita no tempo passado.

ESQUEMA DA FORMA INTERROGATIVA NO PASSADO

Verbo auxiliar	Sujeito	Verbo na forma básica (infinitivo)	
Did	Mary	work	yesterday?
—	Mary	trabalhou	ontem?
Did	he	steal	my purse?
—	Ele	roubou	minha bolsa?

Forma negativa no passado

Observe os exemplos:

Mary worked yesterday.
(Mary trabalhou ontem.)

Mary did not work yesterday.
   didn't work
(Mary não trabalhou ontem.)

He stole the purse.
(Ele roubou a bolsa.)

He did not steal the purse.
   didn't steal
(Ele não roubou a bolsa.)

ESQUEMA DA FORMA INTERROGATIVA NO PASSADO

Verbo auxiliar	Sujeito	Verbo na forma básica (infinitivo) [sem **to**]	
Mary	did not	work	yesterday?
Mary	didn't	work	yesterday?

eighty-nine **89**

ACTIVITIES

1 Complete the questions in the past changing the main verb to the base form.

a)	The boys	played	football yesterday.
	Did the boys	play	football yesterday?
b)	The people	helped	Mrs Green.
	_____ the people	_____	Mrs Green?
c)	John	lived	in France last year.
	_____ John	_____	in France last year?
d)	They	worked	in a big factory.
	_____ they	_____	in a big factory?

2 Attention! When the sentence is negative, use the main verb in the base form:

a) My mother		called	me.
My mother	did not	call	me.
My mother	didn't	call	me.
b) She		wanted	to drink a cup of coffee.
She	did not	_____	to drink a cup of coffee.
She	didn't	_____	to drink a cup of coffee.
c) She		showed	me her photo.
She	did not	_____	me her photo.
She	didn't	_____	me her photo.
d) They		liked	to play tennis.
They	did not	_____	to play tennis.
They	didn't	_____	to play tennis.

LEARN THIS
IRREGULAR VERBS

Infinitive		Past tense		Past participle	
1. to go	(ir)	went	(foi...)	gone	(ido)
2. to come	(vir)	came	(veio...)	come	(vindo)
3. to find	(encontrar)	found	(encontrou)	found	(encontrado)

4.	to see	(ver)	saw	(viu...)	seen (visto)
5.	to take	(pegar, levar)	took	(pegou...)	taken (pego)
6.	to drink	(beber)	drank	(bebeu...)	drunk (bebido)
7.	to speak	(falar)	spoke	(falou...)	spoken (falado)
8.	to be	(ser, estar)	was, were	(era...)	been (sido, estado)
9.	to have	(ter)	had	(teve...)	had (tido)
10.	to get up	(levantar)	got up	(levantou...)	got up (levantado)
11.	to buy	(comprar)	bought	(comprou...)	bought (comprado)
12.	to eat	(comer)	ate	(comeu...)	eaten (comido)
13.	to steal	(roubar)	stole	(roubou...)	stolen (roubado)
14.	to catch	(pegar, agarrar)	caught	(pegou...)	caught (pego)
15.	to sleep	(dormir)	slept	(dormiu...)	slept (dormido)
16.	to give	(dar)	gave	(deu...)	given (dado)
17.	to send	(enviar)	sent	(enviou...)	sent (enviado)
18.	to sell	(vender)	sold	(vendeu...)	sold (vendido)
19.	to write	(escrever)	wrote	(escreveu...)	written (escrito)
20.	to shut	(fechar)	shut	(fechou...)	shut (fechado)
21.	to cost	(custar)	cost	(custou...)	cost (custado)
22.	to cut	(cortar)	cut	(cortou...)	cut (cortado)
23.	to read	(ler)	read	(leu...)	read (lido)

3 Attention! When the sentence is interrogative, use the main verb in the base form.

   a) You stole my money.   **Did you steal my money?**

   b) They went to the beach.

   _____ they _____ to the beach?

   c) Mary came back at 7.

   _____ Mary _____ at 7?

   d) You found the key.

   _____ you _____ the key?

   e) She saw you last week.

   _____ she _____ you last week?

4 Attention! When the sentence is negative, use the main verb in the base form.

   a) He took your purse.

   He did not take your purse..

   He didn't take your purse.

   b) He stole her ring.

   He did not _____ her ring.

   He didn't _____ her ring.

c) My father bought the car.

My father did not _____ the car.

My father didn't _____ the car.

d) They caught the thief.

They did not _____ the thief.

They didn't _____ the thief.

e) We slept during the day.

We did not _____ during the day.

We didn't _____ during the day.

f) She gave me the book.

She did not _____ me the book.

She didn't _____ me the book.

g) Bob sent the letter.

Bob did not _____ the letter.

Bob didn't _____ the letter.

h) They sold their house.

They did not _____ their house.

They didn't _____ their house.

i) I wrote my name.

I did not _____ my name.

I didn't _____ my name.

j) She shut the door.

She did not _____ the door.

She didn't _____ the door.

5 Change to the interrogative form.

a) You helped your friends.

Did you help your friends?

b) They worked on a farm.

_____

c) The people caught the thief.

_____

d) The thief stole the purse.

_____

6 Change to the negative form:

a) Mary cleaned the room.
Mary didn't clean the room.

b) She worked in an office.

_____

c) The tourist spoke in English.

_____

d) She bought a red car.

_____

e) I wrote a long letter.

_____

7 Follow the model, using short answers:

    a) Did you arrive from the USA yesterday? (yes)   Yes, I did.

    b) Did they visit you last week? (no)   No, they didn't.

    c) Did she watch television last night? (no)   _____

    d) Did you study English yesterday afternoon? (yes)   _____

    e) Did you go to the beach last month? (no)   _____

    f) Did you travel to London last year? (yes)   _____

    g) Did Mary sleep late last night? (no)   _____

8 Observe the pictures and complete the sentences with verbs in the past tense. Use the verbs from the list below:

    to get up – to eat – to steal – to write – to read

1. The monkey was hungry. It _____ all the bananas five minutes ago.

2. Jane _____ a letter to a friend this morning.

3. The thief _____ Andrew's car a few minutes ago.

4. Jim _____ at seven o'clock this morning.

FUN TIME

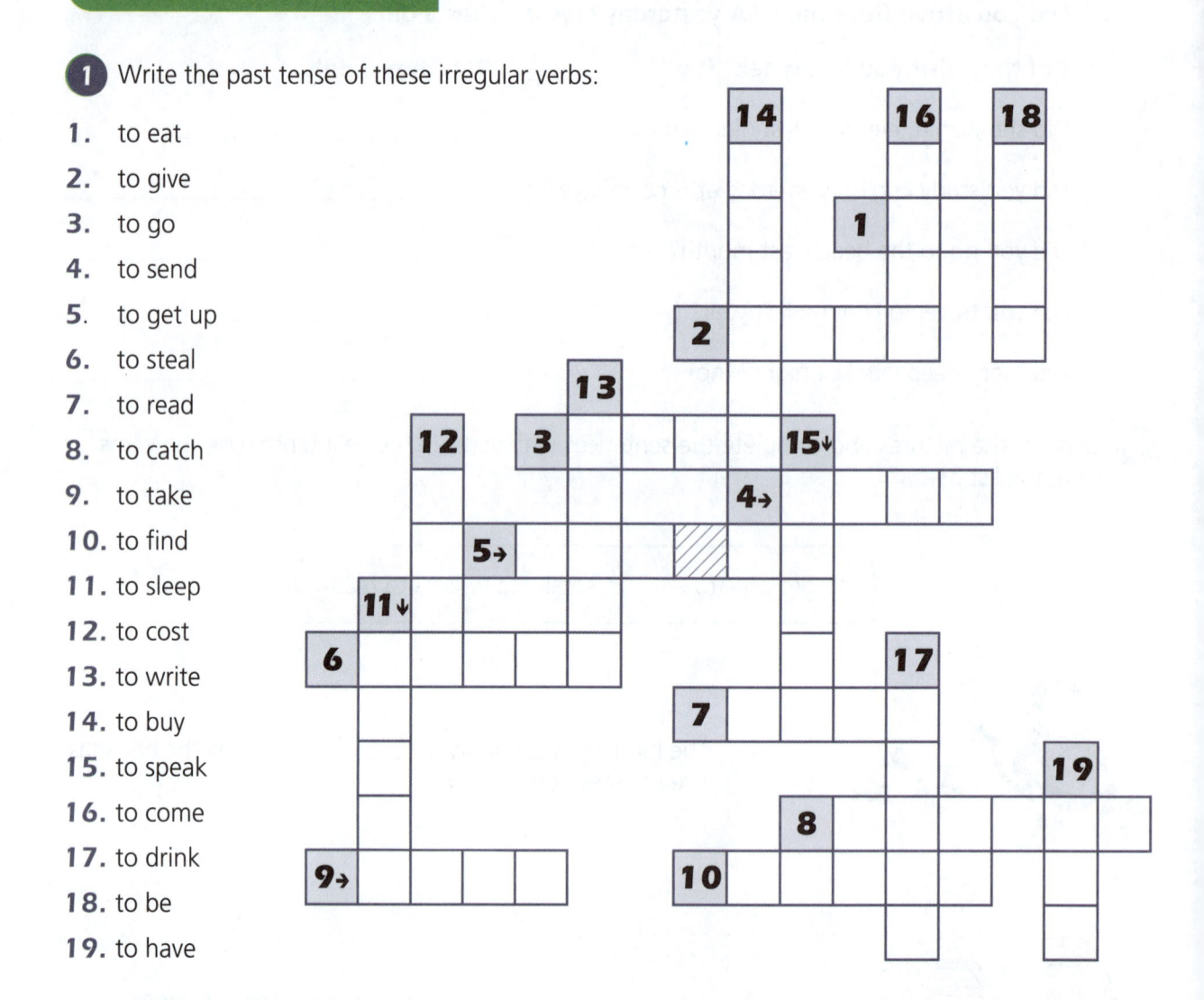

1 Write the past tense of these irregular verbs:

1. to eat
2. to give
3. to go
4. to send
5. to get up
6. to steal
7. to read
8. to catch
9. to take
10. to find
11. to sleep
12. to cost
13. to write
14. to buy
15. to speak
16. to come
17. to drink
18. to be
19. to have

LET'S SING

Count Dracula

Did you see Count Dracula thereabout?
Take care! Go away! Go away!
He doesn't want your blood.
He wants your car, your money.
He doesn't want to kill you.
He wants to explore you.
There are many "Draculas"

Thereabout in the streets.
Don't call the police:
There aren't enough jails for them.
Take care! There are many
"Draculas" thereabout.
They're looking for you
During the day, during the night.

Antes de cantar a música, ouça o professor ou o CD, prestando atenção na pronúncia das palavras. Procure, também, saber o significado delas.

94 ninety-four

Lesson 7

Regular and Irregular Verbs Affirmative, Negative and Interrogative Form

19

Nancy and Jeff

Nancy and Jeff went to the movies yesterday. They saw an interesting film. It started at 8 o'clock and finished at 10. They liked the film very much.

After the film they walked to a restaurant. They wanted to eat something. Jeff ordered a sandwich and Nancy a piece of cake. They both ordered sodas.

After that Nancy and Jeff walked to the parking lot near the restaurant, took their car and went home.

Fotos: Getty Images

TEXT COMPREHENSION

1 a) Where did Nancy and Jeff go yesterday?

_____

b) Did they see
  ( ) a boring film?
  ( ) an interesting film?

c) What time did the film start?

_____

d) What time did the film finish?

_____

e) After the film Nancy and Jeff went to a restaurant
  ( ) by car
  ( ) by bus
  ( ) on foot

f) What did Jeff order in the restaurant?

_____

g) What did Nancy order?

_____

h) What did they drink?

_____

i) Nancy and Jeff returned home
  ( ) by bus   ( ) by car   ( ) on foot

2 Rewrite the sentences in the correct order according to the text:

a) Jeff ordered a sandwich.

_____

b) They took the car and went home.

_____

c) Nancy ordered a piece of cake.

_____

d) Nancy and Jeff went to the movies.

_____

e) They walked to a restaurant.

_____

f) They liked the film.

_____

96 ninety-six

ACTIVITIES

1 Change into the past tense:

**a) Nancy and Jeff go to the movies.
Nancy and Jeff went to the movies.**

b) The film starts at 8 o'clock.

c) It finishes at 10.

d) I like to walk alone.

e) I want to eat something.

f) I eat something in the morning.

g) I see many children in the park.

2 Answer negatively. Follow the pattern:

**a) Did Jeff go to the stadium? (movies)
No, he didn't. He went to the movies.**

b) Did Jeff see an interesting game? (film)

c) Did Nancy eat a sandwich? (piece of cake)

d) Do you want an apple? (pear)

e) Does she want coffee? (water)

f) Did they go by bus? (car)

3 Change the affirmative sentences to questions:

**a) Did they see an interesting film?
They saw an interesting film.**

b) _____
The film started at 8 o'clock.

c) _____
They liked the film.

d) _____
They prefer a sandwich.

e) _____
You pay the bill.

f) _____
She found the purse.

FUN TIME

WORD HUNT

Challenge – How many words about food can you find in the word hunt?

X	C	V	X	Z	B	E	R	B	I	S	C	U	I	T	E	A	D	T	W
N	B	V	C	A	K	E	K	H	G	B	A	H	A	I	R	G	F	S	A
C	X	Z	D	F	U	R	R	E	A	M	O	U	Y	R	E	Q	N	A	V
B	A	P	P	L	E	O	U	Y	D	I	N	N	E	R	G	F	D	N	U
B	V	C	X	Z	T	R	D	S	A	L	E	O	D	U	M	B	N	D	A
N	B	G	B	R	A	D	R	I	N	K	S	Q	F	R	U	I	T	W	P
B	V	C	X	B	L	I	N	D	B	V	C	X	Z	R	T	U	O	I	Q
N	H	E	G	G	A	E	R	T	D	A	U	N	D	C	X	A	U	C	T
V	C	X	Y	T	R	E	Q	B	R	E	A	D	A	D	E	A	F	H	Y
T	C	W	A	T	E	R	R	Q	U	O	P	U	A	X	P	I	E	A	E
A	B	M	I	G	P	L	F	X	W	Q	B	E	E	F	O	T	U	E	R

ninety-seven 97

Lesson 18
Asking questions; giving answers

Why...? Because...

Why are they taking umbrellas?
Because it's raining.
Why is he smiling?
Because he is happy.
And why did he take off his shirt?
Because it's hot.

Why…?
Because…

Why are you running?

Because there is a policeman running after me!

Why are you late?

Because I missed the bus.

It's goal!

Why are you so happy?

Because my team scored a nice goal!

ninety-nine 99

LEARN THIS

Why...?   (Por que...?)
Because... (Porque...)
Usamos a palavra **why** em perguntas e **because** em respostas.

100 one hundred

ACTIVITIES

1 Follow the pattern:

a) **Why are you running? (I am late.)**
I am running because I am late.

b) Why is the baby crying? (He is hungry.)
_____
_____

c) Why are you crying? (I hurt my foot.)
_____
_____

d) Why is your father angry at you? (I got bad marks at school.)
_____
_____

e) Why are you so sad? (My boyfriend didn't telephone me.)
_____
_____

2 Follow the pattern:

a) **Did you read the book? (It is boring.)**

   No, I didn't.

   Why not?

   Because it is boring.

b) Did you travel a lot? (It is too expensive.)
_____
_____
_____

c) Did you wash the dishes? (I painted my nails.)
_____
_____
_____

d) Did you take the medicine? (I feel better.)
_____
_____
_____

one hundred and one **101**

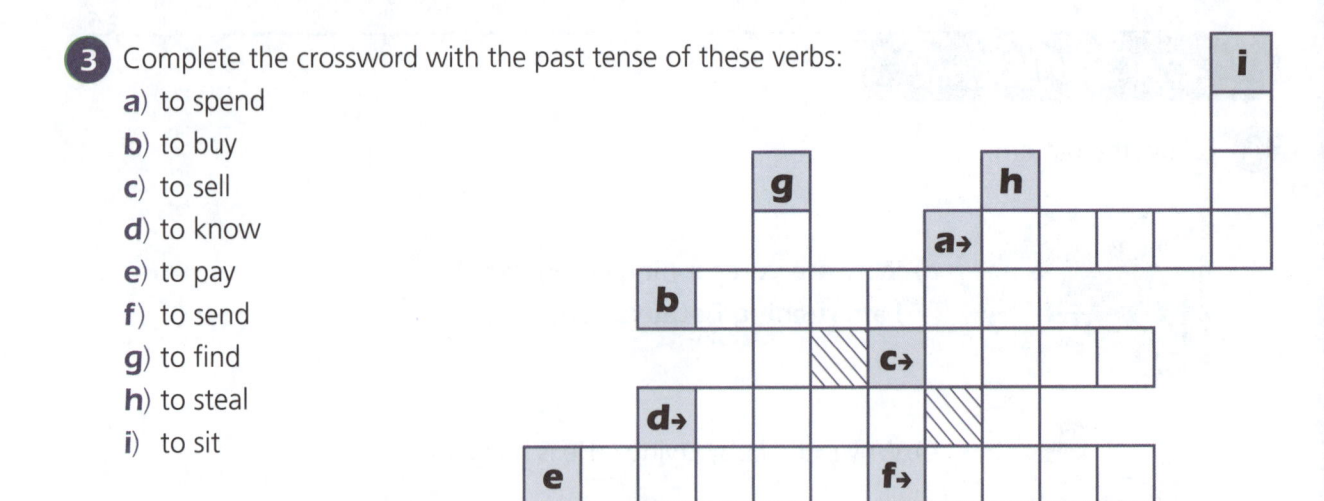

3 Complete the crossword with the past tense of these verbs:
- **a)** to spend
- **b)** to buy
- **c)** to sell
- **d)** to know
- **e)** to pay
- **f)** to send
- **g)** to find
- **h)** to steal
- **i)** to sit

FUN TIME

What begins with an "e" and ends with an "e" and has only one letter in it?

An envelope.

Translate the warning: Beware of the dog.

Come up! The ladder is secure!

I have got a letter for you!

Lesson 19

INTERROGATIVE WORDS

Conversation in a school.

Paul: Who are you?
Jeanne: I'm Jeanne, the new student, and you? Who are you?
Paul: I'm the teacher.
Jeanne: What's your name, teacher?
Paul: My name is Paul.
Jeanne: And what do you teach?
Paul: I teach English. How old are you Jeanne?
Jeanne: I'm fourteen. How many students are there in my class, teacher?
Paul: They are twenty-five students in your class. Which subject do you like (prefer) to study, Jeanne?
Jeanne: I like (prefer) to study Geography.
Paul: When is your birthday, Jeanne?
Jeanne: My birthday is on September, 3rd. Please, where is the school library?
Paul: It's downstairs, near the entrance, on the right.
Jeanne: Thank you, teacher.
Paul: You are welcome, Jeanne.

LEARN THIS

Interrogative words

1. **How often...?** (Com que frequência...? Quantas vezes...?)
   How often do you go to the movies? (Com que frequência você vai ao cinema?)

2. **How many times...?** (Quantas vezes...?)
   – **How many times did you go to the bank?**
   – **I went to the bank two times.**

3. **Who...?** (Quem...?)
   Who stole your car? (Quem roubou seu carro?)
   Who knows the thief? (Quem conhece o ladrão?)

   > Com o pronome sujeito **who**, a pergunta é direta. Dispensamos o emprego do auxiliar (**do**, **does**, **did**).

4. **When...?** (Quando...?)
   When did John buy the car? (Quando João comprou o carro?)

5. **Where...?** (Onde...?)
   Where did John leave the car? (Onde João deixou o carro?)

6. **What...?** (Qual...?)
   What is the matter with John? (Qual é o problema com João?)

7. **Which...?** (Qual...?)
   I have two cars. Which do you prefer? (Eu tenho dois carros. Qual deles você prefere?)

8. **How long...?**
   a) Qual é o comprimento...?
      – **How long is your pencil?** (– Qual é o comprimento do seu lápis)
      – **Twenty centimeters.** (– Vinte centímetros)
   b) Há quanto tempo...?
      How long are you living here?
      Há quanto tempo você está morando aqui?

   > O pronome **which** denota escolha.

9. **How much...?** (Quanto...?)
   – **How much is this book?** (– Quanto é este livro?)
   – **It is ten dollars.** (– É dez dólares)

10. **How many...?** (Quantos, quantas?)
    How many books are there in your schoolbag?

11. **Whose...?**
    Whose bicycle is this? (De quem é esta bicicleta?)

ACTIVITIES

Complete the form about you:

1 What is your name?

My name is _____

one hundred and five 105

2 Who are your parents?

My father is _____

My mother is _____

3 Where are you from?

I am from _____

4 Where do you study?

I study at _____

5 What are your interests? (music, sports, English language...)

My interests are _____

6 What grade are you in?

_____

7 What is your address?

_____

8 Who are your best friend?

_____

9 Match the columns:

How many	Quanto
How long	Quantos, quantas
How much	Onde
Where	Quando
When	Por quanto tempo; qual o comprimento

10 Write in English:

a) Paulo não tem um carro.

_____

b) Eu tomo café da manhã às 7 horas.

_____

c) Você tem que pagar aquela conta.

_____

11 Follow the pattern:

a) **Here are two blouses. One is blue, the other is red.**
 (the red one)
 Which do you prefer?
 I prefer the red one.

b) Here you have two cars. One is black, the other is white.
 (the black one)

 _____

 _____

c) Here are two girls. One is short, the other is tall.
 (the tall one)

 _____

 _____

12 Look at the model and answer the questions:

Observação: usamos **which** (qual) em vez de **what** (qual) quando temos de escolher uma entre várias coisas.

a) **Here are a pear and an apple.**
 Which do you prefer? (the apple)
 I prefer the apple.
 I don't like pears.

b) Here are two vegetables: cabbage and lettuce.
 Which do you prefer? (lettuce)

 _____

 _____

c) Here are two flowers: a rose and a carnation.
 Which do you prefer? (the carnation)

 _____

 _____

d) Here are two cars: a Mercedes Benz and a Volks.
 Which do you prefer? (the Mercedes Benz)

 _____

 _____

e) Here are two means of transportation: a motorcycle and a horse.
 Which do you prefer? (the horse)

 _____

 _____

f) Here are two blouses: One is red and the other is green.
 Which do you prefer? (the green one)

 _____

 _____

g) Here are two toys: a truck and a gun.
 Which do you prefer? (the truck)

 _____

 _____

one hundred and seven 107

LET'S SING

Silent night!

Silent night! Silent night!
Holy night!
All is calm. All is bright,
'round yon virgin Mother and Child.
Holy infant so tender and mild,
Sleep in heavenly peace,
Sleep in heavenly peace.

Word bank

silent: silencioso, quieto
holy: santo, sagrado
bright: brilhante, luminoso
'round (around): em volta, em torno
yon: lá, aquele, aquela (forma antiga de younder: lá, acolá)
tender: tenro, delicado
mild: meigo
heavenly: celestial
peace: paz

List of irregular verbs

Infinitive	Past tense	Past participle	Translation	Infinitive	Past tense	Past participle	Translation
to be	was, were	been	ser, estar	to mean	meant	meant	significar
to become	became	become	tornar-se	to meet	met	met	encontrar-se com
to begin	began	begun	começar	to pay	paid	paid	pagar
to blow	blew	blown	soprar	to put	put	put	pôr
to break	broke	broken	quebrar	to read	read	read	ler
to bring	brought	brought	trazer	to ride	rode	ridden	cavalgar, andar a cavalo
to build	built	built	construir				
to burst	burst	burst	arrebentar	to ring	rang	rung	tocar a campainha, som do telefone
to buy	bought	bought	comprar				
to cast	cast	cast	arremessar	to rise	rose	risen	erguer-se
to catch	caught	caught	pegar	to run	ran	run	correr
to choose	chose	chosen	escolher	to say	said	said	dizer
to come	came	come	vir	to see	saw	seen	ver
to cost	cost	cost	custar	to sell	sold	sold	vender
to cut	cut	cut	cortar	to send	sent	sent	enviar
to deal	dealt	dealt	negociar	to set	set	set	colocar, fixar
to dig	dug	dug	cavar	to shake	shook	shaken	sacudir
to do	did	done	fazer	to shine	shone	shone	brilhar
to draw	drew	drawn	desenhar	to shoot	shot	shot	atirar, disparar
to dream	dreamt	dreamt	sonhar	to show	showed	shown	mostrar
to drink	drank	drunk	beber	to shut	shut	shut	fechar
to drive	drove	driven	dirigir	to sing	sang	sung	cantar
to eat	ate	eaten	comer	to sink	sank	sunk	afundar
to fall	fell	fallen	cair	to sit	sat	sat	sentar
to feed	fed	fed	alimentar	to sleep	slept	slept	dormir
to feel	felt	felt	sentir	to slide	slid	slid	escorregar
to fight	fought	fought	lutar	to slit	slit	slit	fender, rachar
to find	found	found	encontrar	to smell	smelled	smelled	cheirar
to fly	flew	flown	voar	to speak	spoke	spoken	falar
to forget	forgot	forgotten	esquecer	to speed	sped	sped	apressar-se
to freeze	froze	frozen	gelar	to spend	spent	spent	gastar
to get	got	got, gotten	conseguir	to spoil	spoilt	spoilt	estragar
to give	gave	given	dar	to spread	spread	spread	espalhar
to go	went	gone	ir	to spring	sprang	sprung	saltar
to grow	grew	grown	crescer	to stand	stood	stood	ficar de pé
to hang	hung	hung	pendurar	to steal	stole	stolen	roubar
to have	had	had	ter	to strike	struck	struck	bater
to hear	heard	heard	ouvir	to swear	swore	sworn	jurar
to hide	hid	hidden	esconder	to sweep	swept	swept	varrer
to hit	hit	hit	bater	to swim	swam	swum	nadar
to hold	held	held	segurar	to swing	swung	swung	balançar
to hurt	hurt	hurt	machucar	to take	took	taken	tomar
to keep	kept	kept	guardar	to teach	taught	taught	ensinar
to know	knew	known	conhecer	to tell	told	told	contar, dizer
to lay	laid	laid	pôr, deitar	to think	thought	thought	pensar
to lead	led	led	guiar	to throw	threw	thrown	arremessar
to learn	learnt	learnt	aprender	to understand	understood	understood	entender
to leave	left	left	deixar, partir	to wake	woke	woken	acordar
to lend	lent	lent	emprestar	to wear	wore	worn	vestir, usar
to let	let	let	deixar	to wed	wed	wed	desposar
to lie	lay	lain	deitar-se, jazer	to wet	wet	wet	molhar
to light	lit	lit	iluminar, acender	to win	won	won	ganhar, vencer
to lose	lost	lost	perder	to wring	wrung	wrung	espremer, torcer
to make	made	made	fazer	to write	wrote	written	escrever

General vocabulary

A

about: sobre, aproximadamente
absent: ausente
accept: aceitar
according to: de acordo com
action: ação
add: adicionar, somar
address: endereço
admire: admirar
admirer: admirador
advice: conselho
afraid: com medo
after: depois, atrás
afternoon: tarde
against: contra
age: idade
aged: velho
ago: antes, atrás
agree: concordar
air: ar
air mail: correio aéreo
airplane: avião
alike: igual, semelhante
all: todo, toda, todos, todas
all right: tudo bem, tudo certo
all over the world: em todo o mundo
alone: sozinho(a)
along: ao longo
a lot of: muito, uma porção de
aloud: em voz alta
also: também
always: sempre
amusement: diversão
and so on: e assim por diante, etc.
angry: bravo(a)
answer: resposta, responder
anymore: não mais
apple: maçã
ark: arca
arrive: chegar
as: como
as well as: como
ask: perguntar, pedir
athletics: atletismo
at: em, no, na
at home: em casa
at night: à noite
attend: frequentar
attentively: atentamente
attractive: atraente
at your disposal: à sua disposição
eggplant: berinjela
available: disponível
avoid: evitar

B

baby: bebê
backstroke: nado de costas
backyard: quintal
bad: ruim, mau
badly: mal, pessimamente
bag: mala, sacola, bolsa
baggage: bagagem
banknote: papel moeda
bark: latir
basket: cesta
bath: banho
bathroom: banheiro
beach: praia
beaches: praias
beans: feijão
bear: urso
beautiful: bonito(a)
because: porque
become: tornar-se
bed: cama

bedroom: quarto de dormir
beef: bife
beer: cerveja
before: antes
behind: atrás de
believe: acreditar
begin: começar
being: ser
belong: pertencer
below: abaixo
belt: cinta, cinto
bench: banco
best: o melhor
better: melhor
between: entre (dois)
beware!: cuidado!
big: grande
bill: conta
bird: pássaro
birthday: aniversário
biscuit: biscoito, bolacha
black: preto(a)
blanks: espaços
blind: cego(a)
blond: loiro(a)
blouse: blusa
blue: azul
bold: negrito
bone: osso
boring: maçante, enfadonho
borrow: pedir emprestado
both: ambos(as)
bottle: garrafa
bottom: fundo
bought: comprou, comprado
bowling: boliche
box: caixa; quadro
boxing: pugilismo
boyfriend: namorado
bread: pão
breakfast: café da manhã
breathe: respirar
bring: trazer
broken: quebrado(a)
brother: irmão
brown: marrom
brunette: moreno(a)

brush: escova, escovar
burn: queimar
burning: queimada
bus: ônibus
busy: atarefado(a), ocupado(a)
but: mas
buy: comprar
by: por, de

C

cabbage: repolho
cake: bolo
call: chamar, telefonar
can: posso, pode...
can't: não posso, não pode...
cards: cartas, baralho
care: cuidar, cuidado
carnation: cravo
carrot: cenoura
carry: carregar
cat: gato
catch: pegar, agarrar
chair: cadeira
challenge: desafio
change: mudar, trocar; troco
charge: carga, despesa, cobrar
cheap: barato
cheese: queijo
chicken: frango
child: criança
children: crianças; filhos
chimney: chaminé
church: igreja
chess: jogo de xadrez
city: cidade
classmate: colega de classe
clean: limpo, limpar
cleaner: aspirador de pó
clerk: empregado, balconista
clock: relógio
clothes: roupas
clothes line: varal
clown: palhaço
coat: paletó
coconut: coco
coffee: café
coin: moeda

cold: frio
comb: pente, pentear
come: vir
come back: voltar
come in: entrar
come up: subir
comfort: confortar, conforto
communicate: comunicar-se, comunicar
computer: computador
complain: queixar-se
complaint: queixa
conceited: convencido
confess: confessar
connect: ligar, conectar
contact: contato, contatar
cook: cozinhar; cozinheiro(a)
cord: corda, fio
corn: grão, milho
costume: traje, roupa
could: podia, pôde...
country: país; campo, interior
course: curso
of course: naturalmente, claro
cow: vaca
cross out: cruzar, riscar
cry: gritar, chorar
cucumber: pepino
cup: xícara
custom: costume, hábito
cut: cortar
cycling: ciclismo

D

daughter: filha
daily: diário
damn!: maldito, maldição
dangerous: perigoso
dance: dançar
data: dados
day: dia
a day: por dia
deaf: surdo
debt: débito, dívida
deforestation: desmatamento
delicious: delicioso
deliver: entregar
dentist's: consultóriorio dentário

describe: descrever
desk: carteira
desperate: desesperado
dessert: sobremesa
destroy: destruir
diamond: diamante
difficult: difícil
difficulty: dificuldade
diligent: ativo(a), prestativo(a), aplicado(a)
dinner: jantar
dining room: sala de jantar
directly: diretamente
dirty: sujo(a)
disappear: desaparecer
dish: travessa, prato
disobey: desobedecer
disposal: disposição
disturb: perturbar
do: fazer
do the dishes: lavar a louça
doctor: médico(a)
doctor's: consultório médico
dog: cão
doll: boneca
door: porta
draw: desenhar
drawing: desenho
dress: vestido
drill: treino, exercício
drink: beber, bebida
drive: dirigir
driver: motorista
dry: seco
drugstore: farmácia, drogaria
dumb: mudo(a)

E

each: cada
each other: um ao outro
early: cedo
Earth: Terra
easy: fácil
eat: comer

egg: ovo
eggplant: berinjela
embrace: abraçar
employ: empregar
end: fim, terminar
England: Inglaterra
English: inglês
enjoy: aproveitar, usufruir, divertir
entirely: inteiramente
envious: invejoso(a)
environment: meio ambiente
evening: tarde, anoitecer
ever: sempre
every: cada
everywhere: por toda a parte
excuse me: desculpe-me
expensive: caro(a)
explain: explicar
eye: olho

F

factory: fábrica
false: falso(a)
far: longe
farm: fazenda
fashion: moda
fast: rápido(a)
feed: alimentar
feel: sentir, sentir-se
fellow: colega, companheiro(a)
fence: cerca
few: poucos
fig: figo
fill in: preencher
finally: finalmente
find: encontrar
find out: descobrir
finger: dedo
finish: terminar
first: primeiro(a)
first of all: antes de tudo
fish: peixe; pescar
flag: bandeira
flat: apartamento
follow: seguir
following: seguinte
flower: flor

food: alimento, comida
foot: pé
for: para, por
for example: por exemplo
forget: esquecer
found: achado, achados
fox: raposa
freedom: liberdade
French: francês
French fries: batatas fritas
Frenchman: francês
fresh: fresco
friend: amigo(a)
friendly: amigável, afável
friendship: amizade
from: de (origem), desde
lost and found: achados e perdidos
fun: graça, divertimento, brincadeira

G

game: jogo
garbage: lixo
generally: geralmente
garlic: alho
get: conseguir, chegar, adquirir
get away: escapar
get up: levantar
giant: gigante
girl: menina, garota, moça
girlfriend: namorada
give: dar
give up: desistir
glass: copo; vidro
glasses: copos; óculos
glue: colar, cola
go: ir
goat: cabra
God: Deus
gold: ouro
good: bom, boa
go out: sair
go to bed: ir dormir
grade: grau, série
grass: grama
great: grande, ótimo
green: verde
gun: espingarda; arma, revólver

H

hair: cabelo
ham: presunto
hand: mão
handsome: simpático, bonito, elegante
happy: feliz
hard: duro, pesado (a)
hardly ever: dificilmente
hat: chapéu
hate: detestar
have: ter
health: saúde
healthy: saudável
hear: escutar, ouvir
hearing: de ouvir, de escutar
heavy: pesado(a)
help: ajudar; socorro
helpful: proveitoso, útil
hen: galinha
her: dela, para ela
here: aqui
hers: dela
hidden: oculto(a), escondido(a)
high: alto(a)
him: para ele, lhe
his: dele
hobby: passatempo
hole: buraco, abertura
home: casa, lar
homework: lição de casa
horse: cavalo
hot: quente
house: casa
how: como
how are you?: como você vai?
how long...?: quanto tempo...?; a que distância...?
how many: quantos(as)
how much: quanto
how often: com que frequência
how tall: que altura
humble: humilde
hundred: cem
hungry: com fome, faminto(a)
hunt: caçar
hunter: caçador(a)
hurt: machucar

I

ice cream: sorvete
idea: ideia
I'd like (I would like): eu gostaria
if: se
I'm: eu sou, eu estou
I'm cold: eu estou com frio
impolite: rude, grosseiro(a)
in front of: na frente de
insert: inserir, introduzir
interest: interesse
interview: entrevista, entrevistar
invent: inventar
invitation: convite
invite: convidar
it: ele, ela (neutro)
it: o, a, -lo, -la
its: dele, dela(neutro)
it's going: vai
it's yours: é seu

J

Japanese: japonês
jealous: invejoso(a)
job: emprego, trabalho
joke: piada, anedota
juice: suco
jump: pular
just: justo, exatamente
just now: agora mesmo

K

key: chave; teclado
keypal: correspondente, amigo da internet
kill: matar
kind: espécie, tipo; bondoso(a)
kiss: beijar; beijo
kitchen: cozinha
knife: faca
knives: facas
know: conhecer, saber

L

ladder: escada
land: terra

landscape: paisagem
language: língua, linguagem
large: grande, espaçoso(a)
lake: lago
late: tarde; atrasado(a)
last: último; durar
law: lei
lawyer: advogado(a)
lazy: preguiçoso(a)
leaf: folha
leaves: folhas
learn: aprender, aprenda
left: esquerdo, esquerda
letter: carta; letra
lettuce: alface
let's: vamos
let's go: vamos
liar: mentiroso(a)
library: biblioteca
lie: mentir; mentira
life: vida, erguer
lift: levantar
like: gostar
like: como (comparativo)
line: linha, fio
listen: ouvir
little: pequeno; pouco
live: morar, viver
living room: sala de estar
long: longo
look: olhar
look at: olhar para
look for: procurar
lose: perder
lost: perdido, perdidos
lot (a lot): muito
love: amar; amor
loud: alto (som, voz)
lovely: amável
lunch: almoço

M

macaw: arara
mad: doido(a), louco(a)
magazine: revista
main: principal
make: fazer, fabricar; marca

man: homem
manioc: mandioca
many: muitos(as)
mark: nota
market: mercado
marry: casar
match: partida; combinar, unir
math: matemática
matter: assunto, problema
may: posso, pode...
me: me, mim, para mim
meal: refeição
mean: meio; significar
meaning: significado
meat: carne
medicine: remédio
meet: encontrar (pessoas)
men: homens
mend: consertar
menu: cardápio
message: mensagem
midday: meio-dia
middle: meio, metade
midnight: meia-noite
milk: leite; ordenhar
mine: meu, minha
miss: senhorita; perder
missing: que falta
mom: mamãe, mãe
Monday: segunda-feira
money: dinheiro
monkey: macaco
month: mês
more: mais
most: mais
most of: a maior parte
morning: manhã
mountain: montanha
mouse: rato
move: mudar

movies: cinema
Mr (Mister): senhor
Mrs (Mistress): senhora
must: preciso, deve
must not (mustn´t): não deve...
my: meu, minha

N

nail: unha
name: nome; nomear
nature: natureza
near: perto
need: preciso, precisa...
neither: nem
new: novo(a)
news: notícia
newspaper: jornal
never: nunca
next: próximo(a)
nice: belo(a), bom, ótimo(a)
night: noite
no: não; nenhum
Noah: Noé
noise: barulho
noon: meio-dia
noun: nome
nor: e não, também não, nem
not: não
nothing: nada
now: agora
now and then: de vez em quando
number: número

O

obey: obedecer
odd: estranho, diferente, ímpar
of: de
of course: naturalmente, claro
offer: oferecer; oferta
office: escritório
often: frequentemente
oil: óleo
old: velho
oldest: mais velho
old-fashioned clothes: roupas fora de moda

on: em, no, na, a/ao, sobre...
once: uma vez; certa vez
on foot: a pé
onion: cebola
only: somente
on the right: à direita
on time: dentro do horário
open: abrir; aberto
opportunity: oportunidade
opposite: oposto, autônimo
orange: laranja
order: ordem; encomendar, pedir
orange juice: suco de laranja
other: outro, outra
otherwise: de outra forma
our: nosso, nossa
outdoor: ao ar livre, do lado de fora
over: acima
over there: lá
own: próprio(a)

P

packet: pacote
paint: pintar
pan: panela
papaya: mamão
parents: pais
parking lot: estacionamento
party: festa
pattern: modelo
pay: pagar
pay attention: preste atenção
pea: ervilha
peace: paz
peach: pêssego
pear: pêra
peel: descascar
pen: caneta
pen-friend: amigo por correspondência
people: povo, pessoas
pick up: pegar
picture: figura, quadro, pintura
pie: torta
piece: pedaço
pig: porco
pineapple: abacaxi
place: lugar

play: jogar, brincar; tocar instrumento musical
pleasure: prazer
pocket: bolso
point: apontar
policeman: policial
police station: delegacia
polluted: poluído
pollution: poluição
poor: pobre
pop music: música popular
porter: carregador
postcard: cartão-postal
post-office: correio
potato: batata
practice: praticar
prefer: preferir
prisoner: preso(a), prisioneiro(a)
pupil: aluno(a)
purse: bolsa
put: pôr

Q

question: pergunta, questão

R

rabbit: coelho
rain: chuva, chover
raise: criar, levantar, suspender
rarely: raramente
read: ler
reason: razão, motivo
receive: receber
recreate: recriar
red: vermelho
redeemer: redentor
refer: referir-se
relatives: parentes
reliable: seguro, digno de confiança
remarkable: notável
remember: lembrar
repair: consertar
research: pesquisa
rest: descansar, descanso
return: voltar
rice: arroz
rich: rico

right: direito, direita
ring: anel, tocar campainha, tocar sino
river: rio
road: estrada
rock: rocha; tipo de música
role-play: encenação
Rome: Roma (capital da Itália)
room: sala
rope: corda
round: redondo(a)
routine: rotina
row: fila; remar
rude: rude
rule: regra, norma
run: correr

S

sad: triste
said: disse, falou
same: mesmo(a)
Saturday: sábado
sausage: salsicha
save: salvar, economizar
say: dizer, falar
school: escola
schoolbag: mala de escola, mochila
score: marcar ponto em jogo
second: segundo(a)
secret: segredo, secreto
section: seção
see: ver
selfish: egoísta
seldom: raramente
sell: vender
send: enviar
service: serviço
set: pôr, colocar; aparelho
several: vários
sheep: ovelha
sheet: lençol
shelf: estante, prateleira
ship: navio
shirt: camisa
shoes: sapatos
shop: loja
shoppings: lojas
short: curto; baixo

shout: gritar
show: mostrar; espetáculo
shower: banho de chuveiro
shut: fechar
sick: doente
sidewalk: calçada
sign: assinar, sinal
singer: cantor(a)
silver: prata
sing: cantar
sister: irmã
sit: sentar
sitting: sentado, sentando
sixty: sessenta
sleep: dormir
slippery: escorregadio, liso
slowly: devagar, vagarosamente
small: pequeno(a)
smell: cheirar
smile: sorrir
smoke: fumaça
snake: cobra
so: tão, bastante
soap: sabão
soap-opera: novela
soil: solo
so many: tantos(as)
some: algum, alguns, algum, algumas
something: algo, alguma coisa
sometimes: algumas vezes
song: coreto
soup: sopa
source: fonte
south: sul
speak: falar
speak up: falar alto
spend: passar, gastar
spinach: espinafre
spot: assinalar, mancar

square: quadrado, praça, quadra
stand: banca, permanecer
stand up: ficar de pé
start: começar
state: estado
stay: ficar
steak: bife
steal: roubar
stole: roubou
stone: pedra
stop: parar
stores: armazéns, depósitos, lojas
story: história
street: rua
study: estudar
studies: estudos
substitute: substituir
suffer: sofrer
subject: sujeito, assunto
such as: assim como
Sugar Loaf: Pão de Açúcar (Rio)
suggest: sugerir
Sun: Sol
Sunday: domingo
sure: com certeza
sweep: varrer
sweet: doce
swim: nadar
swimmer: nadador(a)
swimming: natação
swimming pool: piscina

T

table: mesa
table tennis: tênis de mesa
tail: rabo
take: pegar, levar
take off: subir, tirar
take part: participar, tomar parte

118 one hundred and eighteen

talk: conversar
tall: alto(a)
tallest: mais alto
tea: chá
team: time
teeth: dentes
tell: contar, dizer, falar
that: aquele(a), aquilo
their: deles, delas
them: os, as, -los, -las
then: então, depois
these: estes, estas
thief: ladrão
thin: magro, fino
thing: coisa
think: pensar
third: terceiro(a)
thirsty: com sede, sedento(a)
this: este, esta, isto
those: aqueles, aquelas
through: através de
throw: jogar, arremessar
time: tempo
times: vezes, tempos
tired: cansado(a)
to: para, a
today: hoje
tomato: tomate
tomorrow: amanhã
too: também, demais
touch: tocar
tour: roteiro, passeio
tour agency: agência de turismo
tourist: turista
toy: brinquedo
traffic accident: acidente de tráfego
train: trem
travel: viajar; viagem
tree: árvore

trousers: calça
truck: caminhão
truth: verdade
true: verdadeiro
try: tentar, experimentar
turn off: desligar
twice: duas vezes
type: datilografar

U

umbrella: guarda-chuva, sombrinha
under: debaixo
underline: sublinhar
understand: compreender, entender
unscramble: desembaralhar
until: até
untruthful: falso
up: para cima
use: usar
usually: geralmente

V

vacation: férias
vegetable: legume
very: muito
very much: muitíssimo
village: vila
visit: visitar
vivid: vívido
vowel: vogal

W

wait: esperar
walk: caminhar, andar
wallet: carteira
want: querer, desejar
warning: aviso, advertência
was: era, estava...
wash: lavar

waste: lixo, resíduos
wastebasket: cesta de lixo
watch: assistir; relógio.
watching birds: observando pássaros
water: água; regar
waterfall: cachoeira
way: caminho, modo
weak: fraco(a)
wealth: riqueza
wealthy: rico(a), opulento(a)
weather: tempo (atmosférico)
wear: usar (roupa)
week: semana
weekend: fim de semana
weight: pesar
well: bem
were: eram, estavam...
wet: úmido(a), molhado(a)
what: o que, qual
what's the mater?: qual o problema?
what fun time!: que divertido!
wheat: trigo
wheel: roda
when: quando
where: onde
where are you from?: de onde você é?
which: qual
white: branco(a)
who: quem, que
whose: de quem
why: por quê

wife: esposa
window: janela
wine: vinho
with: com
without: sem
woman: mulher
women: mulheres
wonder: maravilhoso(a)
wonderful: maravilhoso(a)
word: palavra
word hunt: caça-palavras
work: trabalhar, trabalho
workers: trabalhador
world: mundo
wrist: pulso
wrist watch: relógio de pulso
write: escrever
wrong: errado(a)

Y

year: ano
yellow: amarelo(a)
yes: sim
yesterday: ontem
you: você, vocês
young: jovem
your: seu, sua, seus, suas, teu, tua, teus, tuas
you're right: você está certo
you're wrong: você está errado
yourself: você mesmo(a)